HOW SUCCESSFUL TEAMS WORK

How
Successful
Teams
Work

WHAT SCIENCE SAYS ABOUT
LEADERSHIP AND
HIGH-PERFORMANCE TEAMWORK

David F. Smith, Ph.D.

LIONCREST
PUBLISHING

HOW SUCCESSFUL TEAMS WORK

*What Science Says about Leadership and
High-Performance Teamwork*

ISBN   978-1-5445-1140-5 *Paperback*

978-1-5445-1139-9 *Ebook*

For Dr. Anna Smith. Thank you for your loving and patient support!

Contents

Prologue

It's January, and the company's sales team has gathered in the conference center at a mountain resort on the West Coast. They are here for the company's annual kickoff event, a time to set sales goals for the year and to prepare everyone for the challenging work to come.

After a day of meetings and seminars, the sales team has gathered for the evening awards banquet in the main hall. It's a jovial atmosphere in a high-ceilinged room with a large fireplace. There is much laughter and energetic conversation.

Alex and Morgan seem to be having a particularly enjoyable time. Morgan leads one of the sales teams, and Alex is a member of that team. Both are often greeted with handshakes from their colleagues as they make their way around the room before dinner.

After the meal, the company's CEO steps up to the podium and, after a few introductory remarks, calls Alex and Morgan to the stage.

"Salespeople are what drive our organization," the CEO says, with Morgan and Alex standing nearby in the spotlight. "And tonight, I want to give an award to two of the best salespeople in our company."

The CEO turns to Morgan and Alex.

"These two individuals showed us all last year what real teamwork means. Morgan led the most productive sales group in our company, and Alex was the most improved in sales production of the whole company. Together, they established new standards of respect and cooperation in our sales team approach. I can't think of two more deserving recipients of our Most Valuable Team Award."

With that, the room erupts in applause. Alex and Morgan are both highly respected by this group, and many attending the conference are eager to learn the secrets to their success. As the applause subsides, the CEO turns again to Morgan and Alex.

"Congratulations on a momentous year. Now, please, tell us how you did it."

The Secret to Their Successful Teamwork

Everyone at the annual awards banquet wants to be the next winner. You probably want to in your career as well. This book will show you what can be holding you back from being at the top and what you can do about it. We will examine how Morgan and Alex worked as a team to achieve the top spot. Alex and Morgan didn't become the top team by accident. They behaved with purpose to become an effective team. Morgan has nine other members in the sales group, all of whom did well, but we will focus on the successful one-on-one relationship that Morgan, the team leader, and Alex, the team member, developed. The changes they made in this fictional example of teamwork will also work for you. Let's look at the backstory.

After a successful run in front-line sales, Morgan moved into management eight years ago. Last year, Morgan was as an organizational strategist pulling together the resources for the whole sales organization. However, this year the company flattened management and put Morgan in charge of a sales team. Not only does Morgan have a production goal now, but the sales goal has been increased 50 percent from last year. Morgan now must lead a group of relative strangers to new heights, and judging from each team member's past production, this hill won't be easy to take. The team will have to pull together and get the job done.

Alex is doing okay in sales—not so stellar that offers from competitors roll in, but good enough to keep the worries about money at bay and maintain a good work-life balance. Alex enjoys sales; the prospects are interesting, and the products are innovative. Alex feels the job provides autonomy and the freedom to decide how to best get the job done. Alex, like most workers, doesn't appreciate micromanagers who dictate what to do and when.

The real stage gets set for Alex and Morgan when the Big Boss hands down the sales goal for the team: 150 percent of last year. Morgan had no say in creating this goal and is concerned about several things:

1. How will the team react to this increased goal?
2. How will the team will react to having a new leader?
3. How in the heck will the team achieve the higher goal?

The day after that annual awards banquet, all sales team leaders have team strategy meetings to fire up their members to win in the coming year. Morgan starts this with the team by simply stating, "The boss has determined that our goal this year is to beat last year by 50 percent."

What is on Alex's mind when this is announced? How about the following:

1. Where the heck did that number come from?
2. I've seen this before, and it usually comes out bad—new boss, new goal, new ways of doing things, new reports, new whatever that I don't have time for if I'm going to get even close to that goal.
3. Thinking of which, what is my goal as part of the total?
4. I heard Morgan was great in sales. Perhaps I can learn something. Or is Morgan more of a my-way-or-the-highway boss like I had a few years ago?

Can you think of other thoughts Alex might have had? Have you been in this position? Have you been Morgan, and you know what Alex must be thinking? I've been part of this situation many times in sales, and each time I struggled to stay focused on the real goal: the production. That's because so many issues can stand in the way of keeping that focus.

Here's how to create an environment that allows the team to remain focused on the real goals.

BUILD A STRONG RELATIONSHIP ONE MEMBER AT A TIME

As will be illustrated through Alex and Morgan (and other players as needed), the one-on-one relationship Morgan and Alex develop over the next few months is the key to getting the work done. Social scientists call this relationship the "leader-member exchange" relationship (LMX). There are lots of academic papers on LMX, but the science boils down to this:

1. A leader and a team member (such as a supervisor and a worker, or a divisional vice president and a regional vice president, etc.) are a "dyad," meaning two interconnected people. Morgan is a team leader and Alex a team member.
2. The dyad is a team of two. In this book, the critical element is contained in the idea that leadership is a one-on-one sport. Of course, there are group dynamics ("Oorah!" shout the Marines), but that's for other books.
3. The leader acts in ways that can either improve or

diminish the quality of that relationship. For example, asking a team member what they think about their pay scale is an action that, if handled correctly, improves the relationship's LMX quality.

4. Individual team members also act in ways that can improve or degrade the LMX quality. For example, a team member who is always late to team conference calls is likely degrading the LMX relationship quality with their leader.

5. The quality of the LMX relationship is a barometer of how likely it is that a team will achieve its goals.

Understanding how Morgan and Alex build their relationship will help you develop your own leadership skills and increase your team's performance and results. There are many aspects of leadership that could be considered, but research has shown that the factors we focus on in this book are critical to leadership success.

WHY ME?

I wrote this book to inspire others with what I have seen in my career. My research has shown how team leaders and team members can improve their teamwork and achieve impressive results by consciously changing their behaviors. Although the principles apply to just about any dyadic relationship, including those on charitable boards, baseball teams, and other personal areas, this book looks at teamwork through the lens of sales, which I have been involved in since I was twelve (would you like to subscribe to the Oregonian? Would you like to buy tickets to the Scout Fair?). I have worked for many bosses. Some were leaders, and some were managers without leadership skills. Some were good, some were not. Sound familiar?

I became fascinated ten years ago with how team leaders differ and how team members react individually to these differences. I saw the objective and subjective results of the leader-member exchanges. I completed my PhD. studies in organizational leadership in 2016 with a dissertation on the subject "a qualitative study of relations-oriented behaviors related to voluntary turnover intention as mediated by leader-member exchange." Translated: Does it matter how a leader behaves in terms of the outcome of team members thinking about quitting their jobs? And how does LMX fit into this?

If those questions matter to you—and they should in very concrete ways—then this book is for you, and I'm your expert guide. Leadership may be the number one determinant of team success or failure for you. My goal is not to coach you on how to manage. It is not to teach skills on how to lead thousands of workers at Google. My goal is to coach team leaders on how to adopt five specific behaviors proven to improve their team member relationships and bring greater success. These five specific behaviors are easily recognized and easy to implement, measure, and modify. They are in your control. I want to help leaders help themselves. With this book, I believe I will achieve my goal, so you and your team can achieve yours.

FIVE STAR LEADERSHIP®

My organization is called Five Star Leadership®, and this book is a distillation of our workshops. There are valuable resources on the website LMXPro.com to supplement your reading. Our work is science based and backed by evidence gathered in the field. Everything we teach has the backing of many academics in the fields of organizational leadership, psychology, sociology, statistics, and others.

The "five star" refers to Yelp®-like reviews (in social science, this is called a Likert-type scale). Are you as a leader a five-star implementer of behaviors that lead to high-quality LMX? We can test for that. Our goal is to show you how to be a five-star leader by helping you learn and implement five specific leader behaviors that have been proven to make a positive difference on team outcomes.

This book is divided into four parts:

- **Part One** is about the leader-member exchange relationship and behaviors for a foundational understanding of the concepts.

- **Part Two** relates LMX relationship quality from the team leader perspective.
- **Part Three** flips this and is from the member's perspective.
- **Part Four** is a toolkit of ideas on implementing some or all these behaviors. Reading the toolkit articles will help cement the learning and will help you apply that new knowledge.

The rewards are worth the effort. Are you ready to get started?

PART ONE

The Foundations of Leader-member Exchange Quality

CHAPTER 1

Leaders and Members

A man who carries a cat by the tail learns something he can learn in no other way.

—MARK TWAIN

This section will get a little academic, so let's use Morgan and Alex to illustrate the points as they are presented. Morgan has goals and must motivate the team members to achieve those goals. You could list all sorts of problems, describe scenarios, and so on, but the challenge is simple: "we need to meet the 150 percent goal given to us from on high." Morgan needs to keep everyone's mind on the ultimate result; everything flows from that. HR issues such as time-off calendaring, or disruptions such as members quitting, or changes in budget are all distractions from the main goal. A good manager will put in place a plan that accomplishes the goal and be ready to meet the management challenges presented along the way.

Leaders must be good managers or have one on the team. Teams do not run themselves. Those that do seem to run themselves generally have a team that is working well, and there are high-quality LMX relationships. So don't throw away your MBA; that's valuable information you must use to meet your goals. Morgan is a great manager who understands metrics, cost-benefit analysis, hiring, and much more. With that said, Morgan recognizes that leadership hasn't been a big part of the career so far.

When the Big Boss handed down the 150 percent goal, Morgan felt sideswiped by a bus. When assigned the team leader role, no one mentioned the soon-to-be-announced increase of 50 percent in the team goal. The performance metrics show that the team isn't firing on all cylinders; only about half are likely to contribute to the increase if nothing changes. Morgan asked about hiring more salespeople for the team, but the Boss rejected that idea, leaving Morgan in search of answers.

Morgan attends a leadership development seminar. At first, the material seems mostly academic. It's theory. The instructor throws around unfamiliar words like "leader-member exchange," "Inclusion," "Respecting,"

"Rewarding," "Improvement", and "Modeling". Despite the foreign words, the discussion starts to make sense. Perhaps Morgan is what psychologists call an "unconscious competent," or someone who intuitively knows the right way to do certain things, and the seminar is making Morgan think about leadership in a new way.

The workshop facilitator puts up a slide: what's the average difference in score between the top finisher in PGA tournaments and the second-place finisher? The difference in score is tiny—between one and two strokes on average—but the difference in prize winnings is astronomical. It is worth an accomplished professional golfer's time to learn and practice continuously. They have coaches, videos, and spectators to let them know their weaknesses. The game itself does that, too! Winners work to keep their edge and get even better. Thus chastened, Morgan sticks with the workshop leader, now understanding that the goal is both teaching and bringing to consciousness those things that make a difference.

THE ACADEMICS

Do not be afraid. Even if the word "academic" brings thoughts of monsters, boredom, or that college professor you hated, understanding how this LMX thing works makes doing the right things much easier. Just as understanding the parts of a golf swing can add up to a better game, understanding the parts of leadership addressed in this book makes implementation more effective. This won't be a "do this" type of education. This is a "here's why and some ideas" that you internalize, customize, personalize, and use as you want. That requires an understanding of the parts.

LEADER-MEMBER EXCHANGE

Three words say it all. This is about leaders, their team members, and their work-based social exchange. This is LMX. Developing high-quality LMX relationships is how a leader gets others to do what the leader needs done. In *Braveheart*, Mel Gibson's character is exhorting the rebellious crowd of followers to kill the other guys. He rides up and down the line yelling. Don't pay attention to the words; watch Mel's eyes. He is connecting one-on-one: you there, go out and get me some bad guys. And you, and you...

What do you think of the following thought? "A crowd's action is the sum of the actions of each individual member of the crowd." I think that while there are group dynamics at play, these dynamics just affect individuals (maybe all of them), who then have individual behaviors that add up to crowd behavior. If this thought has any merit to you, then apply it to your team. Work with each team member as individuals to affect individual outcomes that add up to team outcomes. Yes, individuals need to cooperate in many cases, but it is each individual cooperating with another that is the behavior you want to affect.

As noted earlier, the leader-member exchange relationship (LMX) is a social science construct. A "construct" is a defined, measurable variable, and LMX is a measure, from low to high, of the quality of the relationship between a leader and a team member. Higher-quality relationships are associated strongly with achieving goals.

A major part of this relationship is the amount of trust the leader has in the member and vice versa. Measuring trust can be a subtle science. Often, we're not measuring levels of trust as much as checking to see whether trust exists. A handful of questions can help clarify trust in the leader-member exchange:

- Do you know where you stand with your leader or follower?
- Do you usually know how satisfied your leader or follower is with what you do?
- How well does your leader or follower understand your job problems and needs?

These questions may not ask about trust specifically, but they solicit information about the building blocks of trust. The answers to these questions fall on a scale—from "I rarely know how satisfied my leader or follower is with my work" to "Very often I know how satisfied they are"—and help determine where a leader and a member stand with one another.

The quality of the LMX relationship you have with a member is measurable. There are tests for LMX quality showing whether the quality is high, low, or in between. LMX quality is an attribute of your relationship with a team member. This is important because studies show that members who enjoy a high-quality LMX relationship with their leaders are more likely to have:

- Higher productivity,
- Lower absenteeism,
- More extra-role member behaviors (mentoring, for example), and
- Fewer and less-serious thoughts about quitting.

Are these what you would like from your team members? If the answer is yes, read on to find out how to achieve them.

TESTING FOR LMX QUALITY

Social scientists use "instruments" that through statistics have been shown to reliably indicate whatever subject is being tested. For LMX, the survey instruments ask questions of the leader and/or follower such as "Do you know where you stand with your (leader/follower)? (One to five)." And "How well does your (leader/follower) recognize your potential? (One to five)." These questions are distilled from hours of interviews, bigger surveys, and expert analysis so that they are useful tools. For example, the Leader-Member Exchange 7 questionnaire (LMX-7) is a seven-item instrument that was developed to measure the quality of working relationships between leaders and followers. Individuals self-measure the level of mutual respect, trust, and obligation they have to their leader or followers. The results show where you are regarding LMX quality as a leader. It is just one aspect of your leadership, but in my research, it is paramount. You may have done surveys such as *360 Degree Feedback*. Same idea. Find out how you are doing now, act to improve, and retest to measure success. Though we will be discussing five specific behaviors, the use of the behaviors isn't the result to strive for. The result to strive for is to have better and better LMX scores—Five Stars! Higher scores relate to better outcomes. That's the mantra.

RELATIONS-ORIENTED LEADER BEHAVIORS

The last academic piece to put in place is about the leader behaviors that affect LMX quality. There are five behaviors for leaders presented here that also have research-based evidence of effectiveness regarding improving LMX quality. You may have had a seminar at some point on Charismatic Leadership, Servant Leadership, or (you name it) Leadership. If I were to name what you are learning here, it would be "behavioral leadership," but that term was used in early leadership models. Maybe *Behavioral Leadership 2.0* would fit. These other leadership theories do have some of the same foundational concepts as the research behind this book. However, these other leadership theories have gaps in explaining how a leader implements something to bear the fruit of the theory. Not so with *Behavioral Leadership 2.0* described here. What you are learning is how important it is for you to behave in ways that improve the relationship. You can behave with greater **Inclusion, Respecting, Rewarding, Improvement,** and **Modeling.** You will understand much better after working through the individual chapters on each behavior, but let's take a 30,000-foot view now.

- **Inclusion** occurs when a leader consults with team members about how to achieve the leader's goals. The inclusive leader involves team members in the planning process for input and buy-in. Members help design how the work is accomplished, and the leader discusses with each team member what is expected and what the member needs to accomplish a goal.
- **Respecting** occurs when a leader treats a team member with attentiveness, empathy, courtesy, accountability, and professionalism. The leader

expresses appreciation for the member and the member's contributions. The leader provides supervised latitude that empowers a member to succeed.

- **Rewarding** acknowledges the member's accomplishments through either tangible means, such as a bonus check, or intangible means, such as verbal recognition of the member's work in a public setting. The reward must be meaningful to the team member, and praise must be genuine and consistent. Never destroy the reward program by publicly criticizing a team member.
- **Improvement** involves a leader helping a team member develop greater knowledge and skills that help the member not only with the immediate task but also in their overall work or personal lives. Leaders should let members know they will help them succeed through support and developing behaviors.
- **Modeling** can occur two ways: (a) the leader acts in ways that exemplify how the leader hopes team members will act, and (b) the leader shows team members how to successfully complete a task. It helps if you can be as good at the team member's job as they are, but you can also find the best practices within and outside the team and share them as models.

Each of these five behaviors will improve leadership outcomes if leaders consistently and tactically employ them with each team member. These behaviors build the trust that is essential to a high-quality LMX relationship.

Relating to your team member correctly makes a proven, positive difference in LMX quality, which in turn makes a proven, positive difference in outcomes. Morgan's outcome is the total team goal. The intermediate outcome is the individual (Alex) contribution of each team member. Morgan must work on each LMX relationship to improve quality so that it is more likely each team member will meet their individual goal. This adds up to team success (and a big bonus for Morgan, Alex, and all team members)!

ASSESSING MORGAN AND ALEX

Let's take a step back and look at the situation at the beginning of the year for Alex and Morgan. Morgan receives the sales goal handed down by the Big Boss. Perhaps the Big Boss should be reading this book, but never mind. Morgan has the goal and now must get on with it. The senior management approach is strictly by the numbers. Produce X and your reward is Y. This is how it has always worked in my career: top-line numbers are divided downwards with little input along the way from each level affected. Morgan knows this but also knows that things will have to change if different results are expected. Attending the leadership development seminar is one step Morgan has taken toward change.

What about Alex? Team members don't always have the

same goals as the team leader (do they ever?). Alex is the other part of the Morgan-Alex dyad. Morgan needs to do the things that motivate Alex to do the right work. Alex needs to build Morgan's trust that the right work will get done. Morgan must discover what motivates Alex, and Alex needs to discover what will please Morgan. They could do this through mind reading, but it is a lot easier to have a discussion if their sixth sense isn't up and running. Much of this book will help Morgan relate better to Alex, but Alex has a part to play as well. A team member must be open and honest with their team leader when discussing the work that needs completing and the other environmental factors at play, such as reward structures and work conditions. Members must focus on three key thoughts:

1. Find out what is important to their leader in terms of the work that is to be done. What are the goals? Why is this work important? What motivates the leader about the member's work? An understanding of this helps with understanding the whole picture.

2. Exhibit appropriate "organizational citizenship behavior" (OCB). More on this in the toolkit articles, but simply said, OCB is the social science term for going above and beyond at work. It is extra-role activities such as volunteering for committees, staying late to help, and the like.

3. Avoid doing things that upset or cause anxiety in the

leader. The easiest example is "post your activity in Salesforce, darn it, I mean please." This must be important to the leader in some way, and not filling the need keeps the member from having better relations with the leader.

These three team member areas of development are important to the LMX quality. Team members with a high-quality LMX with their leader get more of what they want out of their jobs: promotions, developmental opportunities, flexible work hours, higher pay, and many other factors that make the members' work life (and probably personal life) better. Does the ideal team member's behavior sound like the role of a teacher's pet? So be it. The point is that if members genuinely behave this way, they can achieve remarkable success and meet their own goals for their work life. As mentioned, more on this in the toolkit.

SUMMARY

For Morgan to develop a high-quality LMX relationship with Alex (and the other team members), Morgan must keep in mind that leadership is a one-on-one sport. This is not a trivial point. Extensive research has shown how LMX relationship quality is associated with many outcomes. Using the five behaviors studied by Five Star Leadership®, a leader can purposefully modify how they interact with a team member to achieve a higher-quality LMX relationship with them. A leader is responsible for many outcomes involving team members. The leader must motivate and guide members to achieve the outcomes. Members are motivated by their own concepts of reward, both extrinsic (money) and intrinsic (I like the work). A leader who knows what motivates their team member has a leg up on a manager who does not put an effort into creating a trusting, high-quality LMX relationship. And with that, we end the lecture on the academic basis for the rest of the book.

—

The Five Behaviors for a Team Leader

What would your favorite team member answer if asked, "From never to always, how often does your leader ask your opinion about a decision affecting your work and rewards?" How would your least favorite answer the question? This Part Two of the book will help you understand why this is an important question for each of your team members. Keep an open mind about yourself and how you act; we aren't always our best mirror for ourselves.

CHAPTER 2

Inclusion

Broad, wholesome, charitable views of men and things cannot be acquired by vegatating in one little corner of the earth all one's lifetime.

—MARK TWAIN

We can all relate to what Inclusion is not. So let's start with an example of NOT inclusive behavior by a manager (Andy) who has just met with the Big Boss and is now with the sales team: "We've been handed an annual goal of $2,000,000, a 50 percent increase over last year. Because there are ten of you on the sales team, that's $200,000 each we need from you. If you meet the goal, you get a 10 percent bonus. If you exceed the goal, an additional 5 percent is added to the excess. That should get you motivated!"

Asked how in the world they could do half-again as much, Andy says, handing out a pamphlet, "Here is how I did it in my day. I wrote it out step-by-step, and if you want to make the grade, you will follow this handbook. I will be checking Salesforce on these activities in each of your territories. Especially you, Jamie, because you are the worst at inputting your activity." Instructions include making at least thirty phone contacts before 9 a.m., three lunch meetings per week, fifteen other meetings, and one group presentation a month.

A couple of weeks go by. Jamie is finding it impossible to get anyone on the phone before 9 a.m. "Andy, no one answers the phone before 9 a.m. How can I meet the thirty-per-day activity goal? My prospects are generally available after 4 p.m. at their work number. Can we change the goal definition? It doesn't seem very smart to call at the wrong time." Andy's response? "You haven't given it enough time. And you haven't thought out how to succeed. I know this works. This is a my-way-or-the-highway situation for you, Jamie."

SO WHAT?

What's wrong with the preceding scenario in terms of leadership behaviors? Bottom line, Andy was not behaving with Inclusion:

1. Andy simply handed down a goal without discussing ahead of time with each team member what was doable, even if there is little flexibility in goals. Use Inclusion: "How does this goal sound to you? What challenges do you see getting there?"

2. Yes, Andy was handed a goal by a not-so-good leader, but using Inclusion, Andy could have explained, "Although there is nothing I can do about the overall goal, we can discuss individually what makes sense for you, even if we agree to disagree."

3. Then there was no inclusive discussion either individually or in group as to how to accomplish the goal. Inclusion: "Yes, it's a stretch goal. What do you need to achieve it?"

4. The reward structure was handed to the team. Maybe the monetary structure isn't the right reward for some individuals. Andy could ask, "Jamie, is the extra bonus motivating, or tell me what else would be?"

5. Just handing out a "how to do the job" pamphlet isn't enough. Although this approach is a type of Modeling discussed later, an Inclusion approach would be, "Jamie, here is how I got the job done. I understand times are different and territories vary, so let's go through it and see what make sense from your point of view. I may ask you to bear with me on some points to give them a try, but we can reevaluate in a couple of weeks."

GOALS OF INCLUSION

On each of these items, using Inclusion accomplishes three goals:

1. Inclusion behavior by the leader improves LMX quality, which we know leads to better outcomes. In this case, better outcomes could mean a met individual goal, a happier team member, better extra-role performance, and lower voluntary turnover.

2. Inclusion behavior leads to discussions about potential issues, some serious and some maybe not so serious (but still important). For example, Jamie's six-year-old son gets ready for school (well, Jamie gets him ready) from 7 a.m. to 8 a.m., thus making it very hard for Jamie to get thirty calls in by 9 a.m. It's possible Jamie would make the choice to fake the calls rather than upset the homelife routine. That's not a good outcome. Instead, with discussion, Jamie and Andy can find ways to work around this issue.

3. Inclusion behavior creates buy-in, which underpins motivation. Team members will not be motivated to do something they don't see as possible, important, or even interesting. An inclusive discussion allows a leader to help create that motivation. "Jamie, I know you want to buy a bigger house now that your third is on the way. Does this bonus structure help you get there?" (If NO, then it's time for a rewards discussion as well, discussed in a later chapter.)

It's important to keep in mind that leadership activities and manager activities overlap. The distinction is more of how a person manages. Do they exhibit leadership to achieve goals, or do they just manage people without leadership (or with less leadership than others might)?

With Inclusion, the difference between leader and manager should be obvious from the example, and this is a realistic situation from my experience. Many times, how I got along with my team leader depended on how they acted, not any specific job issue. Inclusion as a leader behavior brings the leader much more personal data regarding what is going on. Team members are people and not data entry monkeys with laptops. It is probable in a group of ten, or even with a "team of one," individual differences in lives and experiences will make a difference in individual results. Leadership uncovers those differences and puts management and leadership skills in play to optimize individual performance that adds up to team performance and goal achievement.

SOME TIPS ABOUT INCLUSION

1. Ask listening (open-ended) questions and look for feelings. "What do you think of this idea (goal, reward structure, etc.)?"
2. Acknowledge answers, perhaps without agreement. "I see what you are saying (perhaps repeat back in

summary), and I see how that would be important to you (and the team)."

3. Disagree only after acknowledging. "As I said, I understand your point of view; I might see things that way in your shoes (empathy). However, I still believe you should try calls from 8 a.m. to 9 a.m., but we won't worry about the goal of thirty. Make thirty if you can, but let's track how many can be made and find a way to get more in at another time of day." OR "I see the problem, but I don't know what else to say as I believe that calls at that time are critical. Try to find a way, and let's discuss this in two weeks." A high-quality LMX relationship will make it much less likely that Jamie will fake the numbers or even quit. Jamie knows that Andy is open to discussion and trusts that Andy won't ask for the impossible (just the almost impossible).

4. Take action. The Inclusion behavior is mostly about getting the job done. The result is generally a plan of action. The leader now trusts the team member to go ahead with the task the way they have negotiated. Most leadership work is around the total job and not about each task, but a key to overall success is success with individual tasks and goals. How much direct involvement by the leader is necessary depends on the task and the member competency. High-quality LMX relationships are based on a history of tasks that were mutually negotiated and then successfully com-

pleted. With time and success comes the trust that the overall job will get done and the goals achieved.

5. Be genuine. Inclusion, as with all five leader behaviors, must be used authentically, meaning your attitude is "As a leader, I value discussing important job-related issues with each team member individually. I do this to understand challenges to meeting goals from my team member's perspective. Only through understanding can we overcome these challenges to meet the overall goals. Meeting the overall goals is good for me." If you are into affirmations, that statement is a great one for inspiring your leadership improvement quest.

A BRIEF HISTORY OF INCLUSION IN LEADERSHIP THEORY

Most social scientists do not use the word "inclusion" to describe this behavior. Five Star Leadership® research evolved its thinking about Inclusion from the studies of empowerment. Empowerment embodies two categories of behavior: consulting and delegating. "Consulting" involves asking a team member's opinion, and "delegating" means giving the power and resources to a team member to accomplish a task. Empowerment, then, is a complex construct with at least two dimensions. Although it was easy to see whether a leader consulted or delegated, finding out whether the leader empowered members is vague in action. Inclusion became the term used because it is the actual attitude a leader has that results in various behaviors. These various behaviors can be described and researched, but they add up to the question "Does this person use Inclusion when working with individual team members?" It is observable, which is why I use this term in my research and program development. I use the other terms when writing academic papers because a common language is useful for those purposes. I use Inclusion because I can describe it in a workshop, and you can see whether you do it or not—or it is done to you or not, depending on perspective.

IMPLEMENTING INCLUSION

Implementing Inclusion is a self-management task. You are in control of this behavior. You either do it or you don't. If you want to do it, here are some ideas to consider:

1. Ask yourself, "Am I meeting one-on-one with team members often enough?" This assumes you can define "often enough," so do that if you haven't. Then you can set up an Excel sheet to track by team member column headings: when you met, what you discussed, whether you acted with Inclusion, what the result of the meeting was, and what the outcomes were. Track this for a couple of weeks and see what you accomplish.

2. Write out Inclusion questions before one-on-one meetings. These may be the same for each team member or individualized based on your knowledge. For example, if you are having a goal-setting meeting, put an agenda together, even if it's just in your mind, of the questions, such as "What do you think your goal should be and why?", "What challenges do you see in making a goal of ($200,000)?", "What can I do to help you make the goal?", "What else is on your mind?", and "What is our agreement?" Be proactive by leading this discussion to get to your goal: how is the team member going to get the job done? What do I have to do to help?

3. When you're leading introverts, there is one tip that can really make a difference. One aspect of introversion is the person's need to think about the question and answer enough to provide personal confidence. That's their nature. This confidence results in thoughtful answers being given. The tip is to provide the key questions to be asked in advance to the member. If you ask, "What should your goal be this year and why?" and you want a thoughtful answer, provide the question in advance.

   ○ Two caveats: (a) spontaneous, complex follow-up questions need to be limited because an introvert will then need time to think—you can use smaller steps to get at the answer; and (b) don't just accept a written response (that's not a discussion). Have the member use their notes as an outline of the discussion and draw the answer out further.

○ If a group discussion is the goal, then invite written responses from everyone who wants to provide information in advance. Collect the responses and use them as appropriate input to the discussion (name names if you want but doing so is not necessary) so the thoughts of those introverts who provided answers are shared. In this way, you avoid the trap of listening to the loudest and maybe not the smartest. This type of Inclusion is effective at increasing the quality of LMX between leaders and introverted team members. This leads to all sorts of good outcomes.

SUMMARY

Inclusion is the first of five behaviors we will discuss that Five Star Leadership® research has found to be important in building high-quality LMX relationships. It is a behavior a leader can control. The leader can purposefully decide to change; they can examine current behaviors, create goals for change, measure the change, and evaluate results. Inclusion is important to the remaining four behaviors. Your job is to meet your goals through the work of team members. A high-quality LMX relationship is built one-on-one with each team member. This relationship is trust based and can take some time, but it is worth it. Coming next, Respecting, like Inclusion, is very much based in respect.

CHAPTER 3

Respecting

Kindness is the language which the deaf can hear and the blind can see.

—MARK TWAIN

"Dissing" is the opposite of Respecting behavior, so it should be obvious why Respecting is so important to creating the trust relationship between the leader and team member. In the previous discussion on Inclusion, where we had Andy provide the bad example, much of the problem with how Andy as the leader handled Jamie's issues had to do with both Inclusion and Respecting. If Andy showed respect, then Jamie would have been included in the decisions that affected the job. Respecting is an attitude that is exhibited in leader behaviors. Management metrics are useful in alerting you to problem areas, but how those are addressed by the team leader makes the difference.

For example, if Jamie's productivity took a sudden drop, it is certainly the job of Andy, Jamie's manager, to point this out as the alarm bells go off. Andy gets worried that the team's goals will now not be met, so Jamie is called onto the carpet (via email): "Your performance has been substandard for two months. You are being put on notice, and if you have one more month of low production, you are subject to termination. Now get out and make more sales calls." (Worse, Andy could have announced this on a team call!) Andy is on top of the situation and is managing it; the team can't afford a low-performing member. The crazy goals set by numbers-driven upper management must be met. Jamie gets fired in sixty days.

HOW DOES RESPECTING WORK HERE?

First, an important premise is that Andy would have liked to keep Jamie on the team. Andy knows Jamie has performed well in the past, but the numbers just weren't there three months in a row. How could a leader have handled this differently? How could this situation have been aided by having a high-quality LMX relationship? Respecting is the entrée to potentially solving the problem.

1. Andy could start by caring enough about Jamie to find out what the problem is. This example was kept simple to contrast Andy telling Jamie to work harder versus asking Jamie what the problem is. "You have

made good numbers in the past, so what do you think the issue is?" Yes, it could be put harshly, so imagine that Andy is asking this with an open mind, empathy, and trust.

2. Morgan listens while Alex talks. Listening is one of the best ways to show respect to another. It is also a terrific way to find out information! And it is information that will help the team of Morgan and Alex to move to a solution and toward goal achievement.

3. Respectful leaders recognize that there can be many reasons for current outcomes. These can be personal and private, such as hard times at home or an illness. They can be indicators of other problems, such as job dissatisfaction that might lead to quitting. Recognizing this is the reason to listen respectfully so that the trust relationship supports sharing.

To move to a solution, the cause of the problem must be identified. A high-quality relationship has enough trust to share this information. A team member must know that if they bring an issue up they will be treated with respect. A team leader must feel confident that, should they ask what the problem is, the team member will be forthcoming and truthful. Either way, the leader trusts that when the team member's production declines, they can have an honest discussion about why.

Yes, Respecting behavior is very much related to Inclusion. Inclusion always has respectful discussions. In the conversation between Alex and Morgan, the focus can still be on metrics such as productivity and activity because these are good management tools. Morgan might be reluctant to ask personal questions but is willing to, if needed, find the underlying cause of the problem. Human resources departments can be a great resource for knowing (a) what can be asked, (b) how to ask, and (c) who else can help. It's possible to violate privacy laws, for example, by asking medical-related questions such as "Are you pregnant?"

GOALS OF RESPECTING

Whereas the goals of Inclusion are directly related to member performance, those for Respecting are basic dignity goals. Team members have the right to their opinions, and leaders respect that right and moreover encourage the sharing of those opinions. Team members have problems, directly job related and not; leaders respect that and support the idea that "a problem shared is a problem halved." The USC Marshall School of Business conducted a study that confirmed this adage.

Let's say that company expense rules require employees to share a room when at conferences of three days or fewer. One team member dreads sharing a room due to snoring (theirs or others'), privacy, or just not liking their coworkers to that extent. The member shares this reluctance with their manager, but the manager holds the company line—"You have to do it; everyone does." Or perhaps a better manager, a bit more sympathetic, could suggest the member pay for half the room cost themselves, but they must find a coworker who will do the same to not cause a problem.

A leader would become more involved in helping solve the problem because they respect the member and understand the importance to them. The leader can show respect by actively canvassing others to find someone also willing to pay half the cost to gain privacy. This can be done privately to avoid any personal fallout to the member. The leader could check with HR to see whether there are other ways to solve this; they may have dealt with this previously with some success. These personal and private ways of helping the team member could lead to a quiet solution.

The goal of Respecting is to build and maintain a trusting relationship. When you respect someone, you are more likely to gain their trust. This idea may seem like common sense, but it still needs emphasis here. The American Management Association has extensive programs on building trust, an indicator of how important the goal of Respecting is.

SOME TIPS ABOUT RESPECTING

1. Ask yourself the question oftentimes included in company HR surveys; how would your team members answer this? "Do you believe your team leader (manager, supervisor, etc.) would defend you if someone came to them with a problem about you?" The response choices are usually on a scale of one to five because relationships vary. "One" means "No, I don't think so because that's just not important to them," and "five" means "Sure, that's exactly what my leader would do (and then they would talk with me about it)." Where are you with each of your team members on this question?

2. Team members need leaders to have their backs to feel confident in their work. Respect is very much a part of this because members trust that should problems arise, their leader is on their side and will listen before acting.

3. The trust building that Respecting supports is not about being great friends. The relationship won't mature if the leader and member are enemies but becoming too close can erode this carefully built rapport. Empathy, putting yourself in the shoes of another, is not necessarily the compassion or pity that comes with sympathy. Empathy is key to Respecting behavior, while sympathy, when taken too far, could be dysfunctional in work-related problem solving. Being neutral is generally fine: "I understand the

problem, but you still have to get the work done. What's our plan?"

4. People differ on how they share. Social science scores personalities on a dimension called "need for affiliation." Those with high need, whether leader or member, are quite willing to share to create bonds with others. Those with a low need want privacy and their own space. Not only does this difference matter in leader-member exchange, but it also matters in many work-related tasks. This subject can be the basis of a whole book itself. The crucial point is that Respecting requires cognizance of how people differ in how and why they share. Do not expect yourself and others to match in this respect.

5. Understand why you want to behave with respect. If your job as a leader is to get others to do what needs doing, then having the right relationship is important. Respecting behavior is related to high-quality LMX relationships, which are related to goal accomplishment. You need to maintain your efforts to respect your members. For example, when you have one-on-one discussions with members, ask, "How are things going?" This general, open-ended question may seem like normal conversation, but due to the exigencies of day-to-day operations, many leaders either do not ask this or, if they do ask, do not spend the needed time to listen, absorb, and respect the answers. One option is to make sure your team members understand that

you might not ask all the time, but you have an open door to listen to the answer at any time. Even with this understanding, a good manager/leader watches for signs that a member is troubled and needs to talk.

Antipathy or apathy toward a member will undermine the LMX relationship. This lack of empathy destroys trust. If someone doesn't believe you truly care about them, how can that person trust you? If a problem arises, it increases trust for your member to hear you as asking, "How can I help?" Be authentic. Listen. Empathize. This is respectful and inclusive, because the two of you are trying to solve the problem together.

Remember Jamie and Andy? It turns out that Jamie's mom is gravely ill, and Jamie has been a caregiver these last two months. This situation is expected to last a bit longer. Andy now sees the problem and, while unable to solve the production issue, HR is more amenable to not terminating after Jamie explains the situation.

BACKGROUND OF RESPECTING

Social scientists generally use the term "supporting" for what Five Star Leadership® calls Respecting. The reason for the difference is that respect is basic to the reason for supporting behavior. Although supporting has a host of to-do items, respect is just kind of there. If you show respect, you show support and many other great qualities. For this reason, leadership theory that connects what leaders do with what outcomes they want include respect as an attitude studied. Support comes from respect. People report how they feel regarding their leader and regarding respect shown. Just as delegating and consulting are behaviors leaders implement for Inclusion, supporting is a behavior implemented for Respecting.

IMPLEMENTING RESPECTING BEHAVIOR

Implementing Respecting behavior requires self-analysis. Are you already respectful? If not, why not? Do you care about respecting those who report to you? Being inclusive can be considered by you to be a management task. Respecting is much more personality oriented. If you don't care, that sort of ends that. Fortunately (a) you don't have to be perfect to be a good leader, (b) you can learn to be more respecting as a person, and (c) you can act on a plan to be more respecting. The plan (c) is the next subject; you need to understand (a) and act on (b) yourself.

1. Track the times you have one-on-one discussions and score them for Respecting you exhibited. Use your own scoring, because over time you will get better at scoring and understanding what the scores mean. A "one" can mean you don't feel you did any and a

"ten" means you were GREAT! You may find that your definitions of one to ten change over time.

2. Track the times you failed to initiate a Respecting behavior and note why you did not. For example, in a group meeting you notice a normally buoyant participant is reluctant to participate. Rather than discuss this privately, you call them out. "What's the problem, Jamie? Not feeling up to it today?" You might note, "I did not discuss this privately because I didn't think Jamie's problem was as serious as it turned out to be."

3. Track the times you were respected and when you were not while working with your peers or your own leader. Note why you scored it that way. Think about how that relates to your team members and you.

SUMMARY

Respecting behavior starts with the attitude that you feel respecting others is important. When you feel this way, your behaviors will usually be naturally Respecting. However, it is also possible that while you do respect others, it is not natural for you to express yourself in ways that come across as authentically respectful. You might be naturally combative in discussions, or taciturn, thus not particularly sharing. The good thing is that if you are respectful personally, the greatest skill is listening. Listening is teachable. Respecting is necessary for leadership success, so keep in mind this importance as you continue to behave as a leader.

CHAPTER 4

Rewarding

Any so-called material thing that you want is merely a symbol: you want it not for itself, but because it will content your spirit for the moment.

—MARK TWAIN

BACKGROUND

Rewards come in two basic categories, extrinsic and intrinsic, and in combination. Extrinsic rewards are tangible and are payment for work. Base salary and bonus are both extrinsic rewards. Intrinsic rewards are intangible and appeal to a person's feelings and self-image. "Good job, Alex!" is an intrinsic reward from team leader to team member. Daniel Pink's book *Drive* is all over the idea that intrinsic rewards have become more important to today's worker. That's possible, but perhaps not the most critical point. What is important is for a leader to know that the two types exist, what they are, and how they can be used to motivate a team member to get done what needs doing. Rewarding behavior is the exhibition of that knowledge.

Some academics use the term "recognition" rather than "rewarding" behavior. As with Inclusion and Respecting, the focus in this book is about doing something as a leader. The questions Five Star Leadership® research asked as programs were designed were "Would a team member rather be recognized or rewarded?" and "Isn't recognition a type of reward?" In other words, Rewarding is more encompassing and is how people think about, well, rewards. Companies talk about "total rewards," the police provide rewards for information leading to the arrest, "It's a rewarding career," and "Having you as my child is reward enough."

SO WHAT IS SO INTERESTING ABOUT THE REWARDING BEHAVIOR?

Andy and Morgan are competing. They both run sales teams, and the top team gets rewarded by Senior Management. They have a budget of 5 percent of last year's production for extra reward to be used how they see fit providing the purpose of the reward is to affect a year-over-year increase in sales. Andy analyzes compensation plans and previous production and decides to apply the budget to a tiered-bonus structure such that the pool will be divided according to individual results. Andy's team looks at this and gets to work!

Morgan takes a different approach by using Inclusion to find out what would be important to each team member that could be paid for by the budgeted money. Because there is no mandate about how the money be used other than to increase sales, Morgan can listen to each team member and consider how to best motivate that individual. Morgan is sensitive to the principles of fairness that team members will consider when discussing the plan among themselves. Here is the summary:

- Alex gets to earn extra paid days off, days otherwise unavailable under the company's time off plan.
- Jay wants the money.
- Blair wants to direct any winnings to the Boys & Girls Club because itemization for an individual is required for charitable deductions, but not for businesses.
- Parker wants added days to the sales reward conference in Bermuda, including golf green fees.

All of these are possible, Morgan decides, and because they will have the same monetary value given the same sales results, this is fair. (Millennials are rabid about fairness, by the way.)

Morgan is exhibiting Rewarding leader behavior that improves the LMX relationship with each team member. Which team did better? Wrong question at this point. Which leader did better? Research shows Morgan will do better in the long term. Both methods of reward work, but there are key differences to point out, and it is the differences that are interesting.

1. Rewarding behavior always includes as much individualization as practical and allowable. Later, tips will be given on how to do this in the corporate world. The point here is using Inclusion and Respecting to create rewards that are valued by team members improves LMX quality, which leads to many good outcomes.

2. Rewards should be considered from both intrinsic and extrinsic points of view. As a leader, you cannot blind yourself to the importance of both. A kind, congratulatory mention in a sales meeting is never amiss and might be a differentiator for the recipient. The monetary rewards are necessary but sometimes are just the required reward for work; without the salary and bonus, the team member moves on.

3. Team members must understand the constraints their leader has on rewards. Just because there is discussion doesn't mean the decision isn't the leader's responsibility. Trust is a two-way feeling, so the team member trusts the leader when discussing reward structure. That doesn't mean the box can't

be stretched with innovative ideas; that's a big part of an inclusive discussion.

Leaders who correctly demonstrate Rewarding behavior are more likely to get the outcomes they need from their members. These rewards should be implemented on as much of a one-on-one basis as possible and practical, even if on a group level. Why do you have to be like all the other teams? It is up to the leader to understand what is Rewarding and to manage to make that happen.

GOALS OF REWARDING

A leader motivates team members. They are motivated by both extrinsic (tangible) rewards and intrinsic (intangible) rewards. Rarely is it just one or the other in today's work world. The pride of working at Google is coupled with the great benefits such as free meals and good pay. Katlyn, a new employee at Google in Mountain View, says that she goes into work early for the breakfast and stays late to pick up a dinner. She would have to eat anyway, and this is much easier. She also says, "Isn't the meal plan cool?" Many of her coworkers feel the same and act accordingly. Their leaders probably are very happy with the work hours. The team members are motivated to spend time at work, which is a great advantage over managers at companies with bad absenteeism. The goal of Rewarding behavior is motivation, which should come as no surprise. The surprise might be just how easy it is to do this.

HOW TO BE REWARDING

1. Have a good understanding of what is allowable. Do not promise what cannot be delivered. Argue for expanding the box of ideas that can be used, but in the end, know what is in the box. Share this information with team members so they know you will do what you can, but only what you can. Respect their input about these limitations. Work on their behalf for flexibility.

2. Flexibility might take the form of cash in lieu of sales trips, especially for introverted team members who really would rather avoid the big get-together, no matter how rewarding management thinks this is. However, a good leader can explain why going on the sales trip is very important and beneficial in many ways. Remember, LMX relationships are an exchange relationship that is a negotiation of how to get the job done.

3. HR may have a problem with individualization, and you might not be the CEO. Because intrinsic rewards can be very motivating and not so obvious a cost of individualization to HR, emphasize in your planning for implementing Rewarding behavior the intrinsic side. Celebrate more. Thank team members more.

Create "awards" for accomplishments. Team members love to tell their friends about all awards, even informal "excellent job" stuffed animals.

4. Certificates of appreciation that become part of a member's record are a great no-cost way to reward.

5. Build rewards into your structure that promote improvement (more on Improvement behavior soon). Achievement of certain levels of competence could be triggers for promotions or recommendations for transfer to other desired work. Career paths can become a reward structure in this way and are a great management tool to motivate progression.

OBSTACLES

Educated leaders understand the power of rewards, but they may not be able to provide them. One of the common challenges leaders face, particularly with transactional rewards, is a lack of resources, power, or money to meaningfully reward their members or to individualize rewards. This happens when the corporation limits the leader's options or won't approve a certain type of reward. How you as a leader approach this depends on your relationship with your leader. If you have a high-quality LMX relationship with your team leader, you must discuss your goals and negotiate on behalf of your own team members. Some of the things on your list are doable, and some aren't, but you will not know with certainty unless you discuss these ideas and learn what authority, money, and resources are available. Keep in mind the advice of one of my earliest leaders, Carter: "Don't let your mouth write a check your ass can't cash." Your reputation is on the line.

Restrictions can be frustrating, but leaders also need to be careful not to become so wrapped up in individualizing rewards that they agree to things that are unreasonable. Say, for instance, your member asks to get December 18 to January 1 off in return for meeting a sales goal. You recognize this as a bad idea: those two weeks around Christmas are your busiest weeks of the year, and you need all hands on deck. Giving someone that time off would force additional work on the remaining team members.

A good leader would explain the problem to the member and offer an alternative. "That would make things tough on the other team members," you say. "How about I give you extra time off during slack season if you meet your goals?" You negotiate with the member, and if you have a high-quality LMX relationship, you can find a reward that still makes your team member feel rewarded and valued.

HOW THINKING ABOUT REWARDS HAS CHANGED

Although rewarding has a long history, the context for this book is the modern-age industrialization and management thought on compensation for work. The main point of reference is the introduction of the idea of intrinsic rewards contained in Bass's work in 1985. He contrasted rewards using the terms "transactional" rewards for extrinsic and "transformational" rewards for intrinsic when applied to motivating factors of followers. A transformational leader such as Franklin Roosevelt appealed to moral values to energize followers. Transactional leaders appealed to physical needs that the rewards could satisfy. There was nothing new about understanding people can be motivated by both gold and pride. What was new at the time was the incorporation of using both to motivate workers at the worker-team level. Most leadership studies were about the head honcho. It turns out that there is universality in worker nature so that these ideas of transformational and transactional rewards can apply throughout organizations, including the leader-member level integral to the quality of the LMX relationship.

The two aspects of rewards—the tangible transactional and the intangible transformational—fall on a continuum. On the far left of the continuum, at the transactional end, falls base pay. The member may think of base pay as their due and not a reward at all, but it is a motivator. What's more, leaders may have little to do with setting or increasing the base pay, so it may not be an input to the LMX relationship. On the far right, at the transformational end, are the feelings of accomplishment, the pride of a job well done, the knowledge that someone was helped, and so on. Recognition by a leader of a member's feelings adds to this reward and improves LMX quality.

HOW TO IMPLEMENT REWARDS
CONSIDERATIONS

Here are some ideas to keep in mind when contemplating individual rewards:

1. The rewards should help accomplish the member's ultimate goals.
2. If you, as the leader, individualize a great deal, unrecognized members might resent you and their coworkers, creating a dysfunctional group.
3. You must ask members what they want, but you must also remember that you may not be able to deliver it or will be forced to give them something else.
4. In some instances, you may not want to individualize rewards. You may not have the authority to do so, or the rewards that you have the power to give may not be meaningful enough to make a difference.
5. Rewarding may require considerable work on your part, first in discerning what rewards will have an impact and then in finding ways to deliver those rewards.
6. Remember that rewarding members is about tangible outcomes—increased sales, for instance, or employee retention. You need to build things that you

can implement and measure, so you can get more of what you want.

Rewarding and the other behaviors of good leaders require a three-step implementation process:

1. Identify what you are going to do.
2. Determine how you are going to do it.
3. Evaluate how you did.

Rewarding starts with understanding what resonates with each member. Leaders can learn through casual conversations or by observing members over time. As you get to know the team members—through Inclusion, Respecting, and the other behaviors good leaders exhibit—keep track of what is important to each member. It is their perception of the reward that counts in LMX relationship quality.

As you develop a good understanding of your members, think about what kind of rewards are meaningful to you. These thoughts will give you some ideas that you can refine as you get to know the members of your team.

HOMEWORK

After learning what your members find important, negotiate a way to implement that reward. Some of it may be in your control, but you may have to fight for the ability to individualize rewards or to change your company's reward system. If the summer sales convention is in Las Vegas and most members hate the heat and gambling atmosphere, then investigate why this location is used and think of ways to change it. If necessary, probe the outer boundaries of your authority to discover what you have the power to implement. You may have more power than you thought. For instance, you may find that the sales team still needs to go to Las Vegas this year because it's the cheapest destination, but you have the authority to save money over the next year to move to a better locale next time.

Figure out things you can do on a microlevel basis with each member. These smaller actions can lead to a macrolevel solution as well. Individual needs and behaviors add up to group needs and behaviors. Corporate culture often doesn't support the Rewarding behavior as I have described. Individualized rewards may be considered unnecessary or unsettling and not "the way we've always done things." But it doesn't have to be that way—you can work toward changing the corporate culture. Study the book *Corporate Celebration: Play, Purpose, and Profit at Work* by Deal and Key. They turn the idea that rewards are unnecessary upside down and demonstrate how celebrations at work can rejuvenate company spirit, increase employee morale, and improve a company's financial performance. You can also find plenty of material in the

American Management Association about customizing rewards.

TRACK THE EFFECT OF THE REWARD

After deciding on some impactful rewards and implementing them, grade yourself. See if you chose the rewards correctly. For example, Morgan might create a checklist of all the rewards that are important to Alex. The list might contain bonus checks, one day off each month with pay, or development courses. Morgan checks the appropriate box each time Alex is rewarded, allowing Morgan to compare rewards over time and across the team.

Now, let's see whether the rewards worked. Did Alex's behavior change, resulting in greater achievement? Did Alex value the rewards? Did the extra day off decrease productivity? Did the development course improve Alex's productivity or job skills? As the leader, Morgan must determine whether these rewards are worth repeating. Be introspective and dig down to see whether you got the higher production or improved job satisfaction you were seeking or whether you wasted your time, effort, and money on something that wasn't worthwhile.

In addition to providing data about your rewards system, tracking your results will reveal an interesting nuance—

rewards can change over time. If a member who is single with no responsibilities for others gets married, the member's rewards might change. Having kids might change the desired rewards again. Leaders must modify recognition as needed. Even when the picture is complex, a good leader can usually tell whether team members are responding to rewards. Satisfied members show up on time, stay until the job is done, and thank you for the rewards provided. These activities make for a more pleasant work environment and a more productive, helpful team. Goals are more likely to be achieved.

SUMMARY

Determining whether rewards relate to goal achievement may be challenging. Many of the results you want as a leader aren't easily measured in dollars or units. Tangible outcomes can be more measurable, but it's a complex relationship. Sometimes you can measure more subtle results like low voluntary termination intention, high organizational citizenship behavior, and lower levels of disruptive behavior, but those measurements can be subjective and not directly important to your own leader. Improving the quality of LMX relationships with individual team members is a subtle way to achieve goals. Social scientists may say that the relationship is direct, but it may not have obvious mechanisms. Sometimes you must have faith that the right reward system developed using Rewarding behavior works. The results you attain by rewarding your members for their performance are, of course, a moving target. As a leader, you want your team members not only to perform well but also to constantly improve. In the next chapter, you'll discover how.

CHAPTER 5

Improvement

If it's your job to eat a frog, it's best to do it first thing in the morning. And if it's your job to eat two frogs, it's best to eat the biggest one first.

—MARK TWAIN

Alex asks Morgan if the training budget would pay for accounting courses even though that knowledge is not necessary for the job.

Is it good leadership to help a team member improve at some skill that is not job related? Yes, and by now the reason why should be obvious. Helping followers develop, whether job related or not, is associated with better-quality LMX relationships. Improvement behavior is interesting in this way because it encompasses distinct but intertwined aspects of leader-member exchange. In this case, Morgan asks why Alex would like to take these courses, what they will cost, and whether taking the courses will interfere with the job to be done.

It turns out Alex would like to grow in the company and is very interested in the fiscal management side of the business. The company is likely to go public over the next few years, and the finance area will be that much more interesting. The cost of these courses is reasonable but not budgeted for in this fiscal year. Coursework will cut into the extra time Alex now spends making sales calls.

The bad way to handle this is to use any of these three issues to deny the request. That is the easy way for management to keep Alex from getting what is wanted. This is also the easy way to harm LMX quality built up between Morgan and Alex. One of the outcomes of low LMX quality is having team members who think seriously about leaving the company. Alex has a friend at a competitor who is allowed, encouraged even, to take outside coursework even if it is not job related, so maybe if handled wrong, this issue could gain importance in Alex's mind, leading to perhaps changing companies. Maybe this won't be the straw that breaks the camel's back, but it can be an additional straw.

The pieces in play in this scenario that are important to the quality of their LMX relationship are the following:

1. Alex wants something from Morgan, something Morgan can likely find a way to grant. Alex is acting as the other half of the partnership in negotiating for this goal. LMX relationships are complex, two-sided, negotiated, personalized alliances (like this sentence).
2. Negotiating together and planning together to achieve this personal goal builds better-quality LMX. No matter how easy the decision, the actions that lead to the decision build trust if done correctly. Note that the easier the decision, perhaps the more likely it is that the LMX quality is already high. There is a halo effect of high-quality LMX built from previous task accomplishments that makes further work together easier ground to hoe.
3. Helping a team member improve, even if not job related, is tied closely to improved LMX relationship quality, according to research. The member appreciates the help given, and this becomes part of the total LMX relationship related to other outcomes.
4. Willingness to support a career change is evidence of the leader's respect for their team member. HR development experts focus on this especially with the "job-hopping millennials." They find that supporting career advancement internally is critical to keeping the best people.

It is easy to imagine the Inclusion behavior, Respecting behavior, and Rewarding behavior Morgan exhibits in this discussion. Morgan says okay and says that Alex needs to pass each course and submit it for reimbursement (which moves it to the next budget year!). Alex is cautioned that this is a reward for past production, and if production falls, perhaps this idea will need to be revisited. Alex votes for the company as one of the Top 100 Places to Work on a Facebook poll.

AND MORE!

Improvement behavior isn't just for building LMX quality. In the example above, isn't it true that if Alex successfully trains for an accounting role and Morgan helps in an internal transfer, this is good for the company? Improvement, though, certainly can be directly job related. It is a manager's job to identify areas in need of improvement, perhaps to solve problems or to get better. Metrics are very good at pinpointing these needs, but it takes leadership to act on this information effectively. Effectively applying Improvement is directly related to meeting leadership goals. Ineffective attempts at Improvement can be disastrous.

In our world of Morgan and Alex, we find Morgan being advised by the number crunchers that the sales team Morgan manages has a median sale 30 percent lower than the next-higher-producing team. They pinpoint the problem: Morgan's average business client has fewer than fifty employees, while other teams' average-size client has more than a hundred employees. Digging further, the numbers show that Morgan's team meets for the first time with fewer larger employers and that there is a smaller percentage of follow-up meetings with them. Bottom line, the problem is that for some reason Morgan's team members are not effective with larger employers. The issue isn't total production; the team's total is fine because it sells to more clients. It just makes smaller sales. Morgan's Big Boss points out that upsizing sales without sacrificing existing success would be a good thing.

The team needs to improve in its tactics with larger businesses. A bit of research turns up some history that might explain how other teams are effective in this market. A few years ago, many of the managers attended the Miller Heiman "Strategic Selling" seminar series that directly applies to tactically approaching, educating, consulting, and closing sales with larger, more complex organizations. "Eureka!" Morgan exclaims. However, Improvement behavior is much more than a leader finding a developmental solution to a challenge. Now it is time to lead the members to water and see whether they will drink!

Morgan sets the tone for this at the next group sales round-up meeting. "Folks, here is the deal. Other teams do as much production as we do with fewer new business clients. Our total production is great, but all of us can win if we find a way to do more business through success with larger businesses. I don't want us to change and lose focus on what brought us here, but I do think each one of us benefits if we figure this puppy out. I have some ideas I'd like to share with each one of you to get your take on them, okay?" And Morgan does just that. This is Inclusion behavior time. By discussing ideas that will affect members' jobs one-on-one, the high-quality LMX relationship with individual members allows for a frank and purposeful conversation about an improvement plan to include the "Strategic Selling" seminar. When Alex and Morgan meet, they discuss how much rewards could increase, how the training will improve all their sales activities, and how increasing the pie rather than dividing it differently is in the team's best interest. By the time of the next group meeting, there is buy-in to the idea.

IMPROVEMENT BEHAVIOR AS A DAILY TASK

Managers often fail to adequately consider the power of encouraging improvement in team members. The more mundane the member's task, the more likely a manager is to focus on productivity goals instead of helping members improve. They might train members in a new skill, put them in a mentoring program, or reorganize a team to learn from each other, but they might not. A manager who doesn't demonstrate concern about individual improvement would simply say, "I hired you because I thought you were competent. If you show incompetence through lack of production, you're fired." They may not use these exact words, but their attitude toward the employee may suggest this sentiment in an intimidating way. This manager oversees production without interest in helping members improve as individuals or employees. That's unfortunate because facilitating improvement for team members is the easiest way for a manager to become a leader. Team member improvement can directly and substantially affect the success of the team and help leaders succeed. Modeling is a fantastic way to do this and is discussed in the next chapter.

Effective leaders routinely think about helping individual members improve. That might mean helping them get better at their jobs, but it could also mean suggesting education that members need to advance to the next stage in their career. In the latter case, the training helps the team indirectly. Although the member is working to move on, the help the member is getting from the leader serves as a reward and as motivation for other team members to improve. Leaders ask members questions like "What is missing in your skillset? In your ability? What do you think would make a difference in achieving this goal?" Leaders ask these questions with genuine interest; they don't sound like they are trying to find reasons to fire somebody.

Sales managers often use the threat of firing—either

explicit or implicit—as a management technique. I see it happen all the time. Every January, a wave of hiring notices goes out for sales jobs open due to all the firing over Christmas. Managers who make these threats (and carry them out) do not think about improvement. A leader, on the other hand, asks, "What can we do to avoid firings?" A true leader looks for ways to improve situations as much as abilities. The leader asks the following:

- What is the problem?
- How can you and I find a way to improve on this?
- Can we implement the things we agree will create improvement?
- Can we measure improvement?
- Can we create a SMART goal?

In a sales environment, the process might look like this: break down the multiple parts of the sales process. Look at how simple or complex the sale is and find out where the member is weak. Look for external weaknesses, such as an unproductive territory, and internal shortcomings, such as a member's passive approach to closing a sale. Whatever it is, you discover the weakness together and figure out how to improve. Discovering these inadequacies requires individual attention to the problem and the tools and resources to make improvements. Your team member might need more training or on-the-job supervision to cement improvements. Your job as the leader is to find out what needs to be done and get it done. Review the advice in Bill MacDonald's book *Merge* (and now *Merge 2.0*) for an experienced look at complex sales and how these are negotiated LMX relationships as well between B2B partners.

Through Inclusion, Respecting, and Rewarding, a leader creates a development plan that will accomplish goals. The development plan may not be tied directly to the job. Alex wants to learn accounting to be able to move out of sales. Helping in this way doesn't help you as a leader achieve your goals directly, but you can see how this improvement would motivate Alex. As Morgan tells Alex, "To join the accounting department, you will need a bachelor's degree in accounting, which will take you two years on top of your current degree. I can sign off on some extra time and corporate resources for you to pursue this as long as you are meeting our goals." Now the improvement that wasn't tied directly to the job has become a motivator and a reward.

OBSTACLES

As a leader, you may have a high-quality relationship with a member but still encounter obstacles when certain members genuinely don't believe they need to improve. Many people fail to see their own need for improvement. They may admit they aren't perfect, but they also believe no amount of upgrading will affect their results. They don't see the point in trying to improve. When a manager suggests a seminar, they might say, "Going to a stupid seminar is not going to help." A manager might order the member to go to the seminar anyway.

As a leader, on the other hand, you might rely on the trust that's been built into the high-quality LMX relationship with the recalcitrant member and ask, "What do you think will work? What if we try this instead?" If the trust between you is low, the member will respond (maybe not out loud), "You've got to be kidding me. That won't work." However, if you have built up trust with this person, they might say, "Well, I don't think that will help me, but if you do, I'll go along with it." Even if you have a low-quality relationship, ask what these members need and offer input. Figure out what they are willing to accept. You may receive pushback, but it's something you must work through.

In some cases, you'll find the member has an excellent point. I understand team members who say seminars won't help. I have been to many conferences over the years that were supposed to improve my results, but the presentations lacked actionable information and provided little opportunity for me to master the presented approaches to sales. If your member takes you up on your suggestion, you must make it easy for them to utilize and master the new knowledge. When they learn a new skill, it's imperative that you find ways for them to practice it regularly until it becomes second nature. Yes, this may decrease their productivity in the short term, but the enhanced skills they master will help them (and you) succeed in the long run.

As with rewards, even the best improvement plan may lack resources. You may not control the money, time, or expertise to implement an ideal improvement plan. Some companies see improvement—always a multistep process—as impractical or too ambitious. For example, an insurance company may find it too difficult to take someone from the case-management department and move them through the steps to become an external wholesaler who can produce. The internal training, hiring, and developing may seem too cumbersome. This perception explains why organizations often hire experienced people from outside the company who ostensibly do not need improvement. Five Star Leadership® research finds this way of filling openings shortsighted, demotivating, disruptive, and unrepresentative of leadership.

Improvement behavior relies on Inclusion to solve the problem. By respecting the member's desires and approach to the issue, the leader builds trust. Then the leader uses the right rewards and implements them in a way that should favorably affect productivity. These actions lead to improvement and an increased likelihood that the team will achieve the leader's goals.

The key to this process is negotiating acceptable solutions. The team is not in charge—you are. But as discussed, it's the internal motivators that LMX quality is about. Leaders through one-on-one behaviors create an environment where acceptable solutions can exist. As the leader, you have figured out what kind of improvement the member would find rewarding. Now you have an improved employee who might play a significant role in helping you reach your goals as a leader. You cared enough to help them get better and move ahead in the organization. You have invested in someone, and the direct benefits may be both tangible and intangible. At the very least, you feel good because you helped someone improve.

HOW TO IMPLEMENT IMPROVEMENT

Leaders recognize what skills their team members require to improve. Some employees need better time management skills, for instance, while others need improved communication or technical skills. A critical question to ask is "Can this member get better in these areas?" If the answer is yes, leaders must also understand what they can provide to address these shortcomings. In other words, leaders need to identify the challenge and take stock of the resources at their disposal. It's a tactical plan.

The tactical improvement plan may address the whole group, but you still must consider what individuals need. If only two out of seven members need the improvement and you make everybody go through it, five of them are likely going to be unhappy. After you identify what can be done for each person, determine whether you must negotiate resources. You may not have the funds or the capacity to facilitate the improvement plan, so you may need to justify it to your superiors or the HR department.

After you've secured the resources and launched the improvement opportunity, you must measure how much each participant improved. If the measured change is substantially positive, you will acquire ammunition to justify future company investments in your team members' improvement. You have improved your LMX relationship with your own team leader or the HR department head.

For Morgan, the leader, this means asking three pivotal questions about Alex's improvement plan:

- What is Alex doing to improve?
- Did these things help Alex improve?
- Did the improvement make a difference in goal achievement?

Organizations often achieve goals without going through this process, and this can lull their leaders and managers into thinking they don't need to worry about improvement. This overconfident attitude can be dangerous, especially during times of rapid change that throw these managers into trouble mode. What's more, if they had been focused on improvement and helping their members stay sharp and up to date on their skills, they might have avoided the crisis altogether.

To that point, I remember a cartoon in *The New Yorker* where a CEO is talking with their COO about an employee-improvement initiative. The COO is worried about spending a lot of money developing their employees and says, "What if we train them and they leave?" The CEO responds, "What if we don't train them and they stay?" The CEO in the cartoon sees improvement as an opportunity to make the company fabulous. If you have a culture of Improvement, you are behaving like a leader. You find out what is paramount, implement what is crucial, and measure the result. If you have fabulous individuals, you will have a vibrant organization. A culture of Improvement brings lasting benefits.

CHAPTER 6

Modeling

It is nobler to be good, and it is nobler to teach others to be good—and less trouble.

—MARK TWAIN

Just as this behavior can be spelled correctly two ways (Modeling and Modelling), Modeling behavior has two aspects. It's important enough to understand these two dimensions of this behavior that the first thing for this chapter is academics (again, do not be afraid!).

BACKGROUND

As Bass theorized in the 1980s about member motivation, he kept trying to describe how extrinsic motivators (money to buy food) differed in action from intrinsic motivators (my work is worthwhile). The challenge with this effort was tying the psychological motivating factors to leadership. It's simple to say a leader provides the money. It's a direct correlation. Money from the leader, work from the team member. It was (and is) much harder to describe how internal motivation arises from leadership. For example, there is some evidence that:

1. Taller men with good hair and deep voices, who are fit are described as "someone I would follow" more often than those not thus described.
2. Although a definition of charisma is vague, people "know it when they see it" and can list charismatic leaders such as JFK.
3. How a leader uses words, not the message itself, makes a difference in how the message is received regarding how motivating the leader is.

What these types of observations mean is that no matter how hard social scientists try to pin down definitions, actions, correlations, and so on, there is very little understanding of the fact that people are internally motivated. Pink in *Drive* provides a great discussion that this motivation exists, and so awareness is important. Pink's book is a great start in understanding intrinsic motivation. The problem is knowing what to do with this knowledge.

This book you are reading relies on just a small slice of this debate about internal motivation: a leader "leads by example," "shows the way," "leads from the front," and "won't ask you to do something they wouldn't do themselves." This area of leader behaviors is measured in several ways, with Five Star Leadership® research settling on two dimensions:

1. A leader provides a visible example of what kind of person they want the team member to be. Characteristics such as honesty, sense of humor, hard worker, and so on are modeled by the leader avoiding the "do as I say, not as I do" problem.
2. A leader helps team members improve by showing them how to do the task. They model how consultative selling processes work in action, for example. If they don't do it themselves, they use surrogate subject matter experts to accomplish this as part of their leadership behaviors.

Relying on just these two dimensions of leadership makes it easier to ignore the academic debate and to get to the meat of the matter: how should leaders behave if they want to model for their team? That is the Modeling leader behavior.

MODELING IN ACTION

Leaders model by demonstrating strong character and by behaving professionally. They show how to get the job done, and they do it while speaking well of others, being honest and courteous, and showing respect and loyalty.

Managers don't always behave professionally. Managers may have character, but they are less concerned about modeling it while managing. Think back to the TV show *Taxi*, and you might get a picture of the archetypal lousy manager. In it, Danny DeVito's character, Louie De Palma, managed a fleet of taxis by bullying and cheating his employees. He stole from his company, insulted and intimidated his team members, and routinely exhibited despicable behavior. He didn't exhibit a single behavior that a leader would want to model. (There are some great YouTube clips!)

Leaders, by contrast, understand the importance of choosing the right person for the job. Not only do they want the person to get the job done, but they want them to do it with integrity. The best way for a leader to do that is to model the type of behavior the leader expects from team members. Leaders model how to get the job done. They lead with confidence and enthusiasm. This practice of Modeling is a form of Improvement, which is appropriate because all the behaviors of good leaders work seamlessly together to foster high-quality LMX relationships.

If a job requires a member to be up at six o'clock in the

morning making calls, the leader should be up at the same time. If the leader is not, a member could say, "Why should I bother getting up if my team leader doesn't bother to get up?" Remember, Modeling, like all the five behaviors of great leaders, is about creating high-quality LMX relationships that produce beneficial results. Leading by example is an indirect leadership behavior to improve a team member. The military provides an illustration. There was a documentary about the U.S. soldiers in Afghanistan where a colonel says, "I wouldn't ask my troops to do anything I wouldn't do." This officer leads from the front, which is different from a rear echelon officer issuing orders from a bunker far from enemy lines.

Charisma makes leaders engaging, powerful models. We often think of charisma as something people are born with, but others can acquire it through practice and Modeling. For example, knowing that appearance can be critical in a business environment, a person might model a charismatic appearance by dressing and grooming themselves well. If you dress like a leader, people are more likely to treat you like a leader. You can adapt your behavior to convey charisma, too. Become the type of person you want to be. The idea is that you innately have the potential to be more, even if you haven't yet developed that potential. Look to others as models!

Of course, just because you dress well doesn't mean

your group will model you. Your behavior, however, is one element that helps elevate your team. Consider what happens in an ice hockey game. In hockey, the action is so fast, and the puck moves so quickly, that spectators may not see it go into the net for a winning goal. The important thing is that it got there. The goal, however, wasn't the result of a single action. It only happened because of the nineteen direct and indirect actions that set it up. The setup may have looked random, but there was skill put into a whole pattern that accomplished the goal.

Modeling operates the same way. There is no proof that Modeling provides a direct, practical result, but there is proof that it has an indirect practical benefit. It's one of those peripheral maneuvers that leads to the puck nestling in the net for a goal. The result may not be immediate and direct, but your behavior sets up your team members for helping you achieve your goals as a leader.

PROVIDING AN EXAMPLE

When it comes to training and providing an example to team members, leaders often operate like inspiring guidance counselors. A stiff-minded manager might be content with saying, "It's my way or the highway," but a good leader applies more care and attention. A leader explains what is required, demonstrates it, then guides members. The leader asks these team members what they think and how they feel about the actions the leader has proposed. This communication makes the members part of the decision-making process. Guidance from the leader hones the members' skills, abilities, and confidence to get the job done. They feel empowered and are more apt to polish their skills in a way that considers the leader's goals. They listen to the leader to adopt the new way of doing things.

Remember: as a leader who has developed high-quality LMX relationships with each of your team members, you don't have to micromanage individuals. You know they will get their jobs done. After you explain, demonstrate, and guide, your team member's sense of empowerment is icing on the cake. It frees you up and gives you success at the same time.

You don't have to be the only guide, either. You can bring in an expert who has mastered the task to show others how to do it. This approach can be used anytime during the explaining, demonstrating, and guiding. When you pass the baton to an expert on the task, you make them a de facto leader as well. When you delegate like this, you still retain your leadership role. The team members get the information they need, and then you provide the guidance to make them feel empowered to be expert users.

There are many ways people learn, but sometimes the

task is not adaptable to individualized approaches. Certain tasks must be done a certain way, and when that's the case, good leaders and managers make this clear. However, though a manager might instruct team members on the correct, unwavering procedures they must use, a leader takes the time to explain why those procedures are followed. This time spent explaining allows members to ask questions or suggest alternative approaches. When a leader says, "Let me show you how I do it," the leader starts a negotiating process that cultivates understanding and inclusion. This demonstration is valuable guidance for the team member. The member feels free to ask questions, ponder different approaches, and share new ideas with the leader. The task becomes theirs. They own it!

The leader must navigate the challenge of a member suggesting a different way to do a task. The suggestion may not be practical or affordable, for instance, so the leader must explain why without the member feeling chagrined or embarrassed. A fair-minded explanation is easier in a high-quality LMX relationship because there is already effective communication. Even so, you may have to put your foot down and say, "I understand you think your way is better, and I understand you want a chance to prove it, but we have to do it this way." The leader is the captain of the ship, and therefore is in charge.

A leader dealing with a situation like this must still provide proper guidance. If the instruction isn't clear, the team member won't feel empowered and will then start doing it the way they think is better. That is not the correct outcome.

PRACTICE WHAT YOU PREACH

Members typically won't do more than a leader is willing to do. Members need to believe you, their leader, would be willing to do the same thing you are asking them to do. This may not be the case if you are managing a team of pilots but don't know how to fly yourself. However, if you require members to make ten calls a day, each team member needs to believe you would also make ten calls if put in their position. Members must believe you are dedicated to the approach you are advocating. They must feel confident that this is a reasonable expectation based on what you've done in the past or would be willing to do tomorrow if you became a member of the team instead of its leader.

Say, for example, Morgan tells Alex to work harder and to make fifteen calls a day, and Alex responds, "You've got to be kidding me. That's unreasonable." If Alex doesn't understand the need for Morgan's request, Morgan hasn't utilized Inclusion behavior. If Morgan had used Inclusion, the two of them would have discussed the need for additional calling. But on this occasion, Alex is balking.

So Morgan asks, "Why is that unreasonable?" Alex replies, "Because I know when you were doing this job you only did eight calls a day." This retort creates a tense situation. However, Morgan is prepared and responds, "Yeah. I did eight a day, but I still achieved my goals. You aren't doing so well. I need to emphasize that you have to achieve this goal, which I know you can do. So for now, I'm asking for fifteen calls. As soon as you are on track to achieve your annual goal, let's discuss how many calls will keep you there."

HOW TO IMPLEMENT MODELING

It may not be apparent to you how to model well. The first step is to decide you want to do it, and then you must determine how to carry it out. Will you dress differently? Will you talk differently, or refine the language you use? If you are an introvert who feels like their private office is their refuge, will you make a concerted effort to get out of that office and visit your team members' offices more often?

Throughout this planning, you must identify what you can control and pursue those qualities first. Start by finding your role model—someone whose behavior, appearance, and manner impresses or inspires you.

Your inner dialogue might sound like this: "I have decided

my goal is a higher-quality LMX relationship. I want to implement the Modeling behavior to show my team how to act. I will find someone who I think could be my model and try to be like them as much as my ego will let me." The goal is not to ape someone—to wear cowboy boots when you prefer loafers or to take up smoking cigars when they make you nauseous—but to design yourself in a way that embodies the qualities you admire. A leader, however, can be more direct if they so choose. One sales team I worked on was required to buy expensive suits from a Hong Kong tailor the team lead brought to the sales conference. We did look sharp!

It's not easy for some people to admit they aren't perfect, but if you are authentic, you can recognize the potential benefit of change. Still, you must remain true to yourself. For example, if your goal is to be more likable by putting people at ease, you don't have to adopt your role model's method of using well-crafted joke telling. You can continue to use your own characteristic dry sense of humor that people already associate with you. This is called finding and using your own voice. This is the key to authenticity.

I had a friend a while back who got promoted to be team lead. He did an excellent job. When I saw him next, eighteen years later, he had become senior vice president of a major financial institution. He had always had a great personality, but when I saw him at a conference, his appearance had changed subtly. He had an expensive suit on, had manicured nails, and had great hair (his own). He had become an executive. This process of refining your manner and appearance isn't simple, and if you struggle or you're uncertain how to do it, consider hiring a career coach.

If you decide to change, stick to it. Whether it's buying suits from Brooks Brothers, getting more sleep, or coloring your hair, make a list and check off each thing you accomplish. First impressions are role specific. By that I mean you can be a certain type of person at work but someone slightly different on the golf course, with the Scout troop, or at church. You don't need to be a leader at the golf course. At work, however, you want to make the best impression given what is in your control and what is work appropriate.

Aside from looks and behaviors, you also must model how to get a job done. Say, for instance, Morgan feels Alex needs to have more group meetings with prospects. Morgan might say, "We've decided everyone needs to have more prospect group meetings to get in front of more potential sources of business. We decided on a goal of one a week for everyone. You're doing two a month now. How can we increase that?"

Through Inclusion, Morgan and Alex create a tactical plan

including SMART goals. Alex explains, "The productivity manager at the office who is supposed to set up the meetings for the group that I am trying to work with won't call me back. I leave voicemails and get no response."

Morgan and Alex decide that the productivity manager is vital to getting the complex task done. Morgan says, "I'll call the manager right now." The manager doesn't answer, so Morgan leaves a voicemail, saying, "This is Morgan, Alex's team leader. We're trying to get this group meeting done. Could you call me back?" Morgan also sends a quick email to their relationship manager asking for them to touch base with the productivity manager's boss. Morgan promises to continue following up with the productivity manager, all the while conferencing Alex into the call. Morgan was willing to step in and help Alex through the process to get the desired result. The persistence in calling and knowledge of how to use their relationship manager are what Alex was missing and so learned from Morgan's task-specific example. Morgan could have just told Alex to do it. However, that isn't Modeling and isn't nearly as effective in results. Also, it doesn't improve LMX quality.

SUMMARY

Leading by example like this often leads to improvement. You can do it yourself or delegate it to an expert. There's no one right way to lead by example. The sergeant of a platoon of Marines is probably able to explain, demonstrate, guide, and empower every task they need to learn. However, the leader of a software development team may not know how to do every job of the project, such as coding in Python, but can find experts to show members how to do those things. It is the effort of the leader to help each team member that improves LMX quality.

CHAPTER 7

Pulling It Together for Leaders

The secret of getting ahead is getting started.

—MARK TWAIN

It is critical that leaders use all five of these leadership behaviors. At times only one is present, but sometimes all five are used. Each approach or action relies on the others; Modeling requires Inclusion, Inclusion needs Rewarding, and so on. They're all part and parcel of the total. With all five leadership behaviors in place, you're achieving five-star leadership. For five-star leadership, you want to look at the total leadership these behaviors support.

Five-star leaders develop and implement all five behaviors concurrently. Think about football, where each play and each movement within that play is designed to improve the team's score and increase the likelihood of victory. There are many pieces working together in the game—it matters how well the players block and how many tackles they get. But the ultimate goal of all this individual activity is winning the game.

AN EXAMPLE

Here is what it looks like when all these behaviors work together in business:

Morgan knows leadership is a one-on-one sport, so after telling the whole team what the team goal is, Morgan says, "I will meet with each one of you to discuss your individual goals." At Morgan's one-on-one meeting with Alex, Morgan says, "We have a $20 million goal among ten people. I could average that out across the team for an individual goal of $2 million, but I wanted to ask you how much you think you can do."

"That is how it's been done before," Alex says, "but it doesn't make sense. I'm a $500,000 producer. If all the right things were in place, I think I could maybe do a million dollars in sales, but that would be a stretch goal for me." "That's what I wanted to know," Morgan says. "Looking at your past production, I think you can handle a million. If given the right resources, would you feel good about that goal?"

"Actually, yes," says Alex. "I'm glad we're talking about this because I would have been depressed if you had just handed me the $2 million goal. I would have gotten right on LinkedIn to look for another job." "We wouldn't want that, Alex," Morgan replies. "You are valuable, and we'd like to keep you."

However, Alex still looks concerned. "I've only ever done $500,000. I think I could do a million, but that is a big jump." "I respect the way you feel," Morgan says. "I want to assure you that your base compensation is not going to change. You'll be able to pay your bills and put food on the table. I understand this is a stretch goal."

"But even if I got it up to $600,000 or $700,000, I feel like I would be letting the team down," Alex says. Morgan responds, "I understand. Let's investigate this. How do you think you can get a million? What is missing?"

Alex thinks. "I have a problem with selling to larger businesses; there are so many players to keep track of in that complex sales process. I know the other teams have more success than we do at this. It's not about the products. You know I know the products. I can follow the script, but somehow the sale gets out of control and I don't get the deal. Are there workshops to help me learn how to succeed on larger sales?"

"There are," Morgan says. "So, you think you can help the team by improving your skills, huh? Well, let's investigate that. There is a training called 'Strategic Selling.' Whether you know it or not, you are familiar with the techniques they teach. Whenever you hear a salesperson say, 'Is there someone else that needs to be in on this decision?' they are using 'Strategic Selling' skills. I took this training. I had an exciting time with it, and it helped me out. Let's see if it can help you. I can probably even help pay for it. What do you think?"

"That sounds great!" Alex is relieved. Morgan continues. "Good. After you're done with the workshop, you've got to implement everything you've learned. I can show you how I used to use the techniques. We can check in with the other teams for someone who took that training with me. We could even do some role-playing to help figure out how to make it yours. Let's see if that would make a difference."

"Thank you so much," Alex says. "I feel so much better about accomplishing this goal."

THE FIVE BEHAVIORS ILLUSTRATED

So how were the behaviors illustrated in this vignette?

One of the most prevailing behaviors is Inclusion. It's

all over the place, but we first see it when Morgan asks Alex about reaching a million-dollar goal. With a little analysis, Morgan thinks, "I bet Alex can do a million and even express with confidence the ability to do so." Alex admits to being able to do a million. Morgan is even able to make Alex say it with confidence. From the very start, there is Inclusion about how Morgan and Alex think Alex can improve. Then they negotiate how to get that done.

A manager could have handed out everyone's goals and might have even personalized them. But Morgan takes the extra step of respecting Alex's opinion when asking, "How do you feel about that?" That is Respecting through Inclusion.

A simple form of Rewarding is also present. Alex fears losing the job and money because of an inability to reach the goal. However, Morgan assures Alex that the base pay will still be there if Alex keeps showing up and doing the work. Rewarding doesn't have to be incremental. It can be as simple as reminding people of the base reward for doing the job. HR departments, especially in larger companies, understand the value of highlighting employees' total compensation. When they send out a statement of total benefits, they make sure employees see not only the salary but also the insurance, 401(k) matching, and any other rewards.

Another reward for Alex is the "Strategic Selling" workshop, which comes about through Inclusion and involves Improvement. It's a win-win for the leader and member. If the LMX relationship had been low quality, Alex might have been scared to bring up the topic of training. However, because there is a high-quality relationship, Alex feels comfortable asking Morgan about it.

Morgan also models for Alex, suggesting they work together after the training. Morgan provides guidance by offering to help customize the training for Alex's personality. Morgan might even ask Alex to demonstrate learning by teaching. This approach gives Morgan a chance to catch up on the latest information, too. Even if Morgan and Alex face organizational limitations—maybe there is no budget for training—they could look for alternative solutions given the resources that are available. Maybe Morgan could find other members with experience who can help guide Alex. A good leader will seek a work-around.

A lot of what we cover in this book may seem like common-sense advice, but it's more than that. It's science-based common sense. Countless leadership books list fifty ways to do leadership, but only a handful present material that has been scientifically observed and reported, like this book does. Social science has shown that these five leadership behaviors, developed and exhibited concurrently, lead to high-quality LMX relationships and goal achievement. This book is about making these unconscious behaviors conscious, because the more you implement them, the more success you will achieve.

PART THREE

Three Themes for Team Members

HOW TEAM MEMBERS CAN IMPROVE LMX QUALITY

High-quality LMX relationships are as important for team members as they are for leaders. In the previous section, we demonstrated how Morgan was able to lead the team to accomplish the sales goals by using the five leadership behaviors. In the next chapters, we will focus on the role of the team member, Alex. Social science research is a bit fuzzy on behaviors of members that affect LMX quality, but a review of what has been studied provided Five Star Leadership® a basis for presenting the three attitudes a member can control that lead to member behaviors that improve LMX quality with their leader. I call these "member themes" because these are more a way of thinking than specific proven behaviors.

The actions a team member can employ to improve their relationship with their team leader can be checked against the three themes described in this part of the book. There is overlap between behaviors and themes; many actions can surface from the three themes that I recommend members to follow. However, not all actions come from these three themes; there is much more that can affect the LMX quality. But we have found these three to make a significant difference if kept in mind and acted on appropriately.

Should you keep reading? Many people function as both a leader and a member. If you have a leader, you are a member. If you have people reporting to you, formally or informally, you are a leader. If you are reading the book to be a better leader, the following chapters will help you understand what to expect from team members, and you can perhaps model or encourage members toward these expectations. You also might learn something about yourself and your relationship with your own leader. So, yes, please keep reading.

LMX theory relies on the premise that the two parties of the dyad, the team leader and team member, each want something out of a task being completed correctly. The something they want is called an "outcome." A leader's desired outcome of the member completing a task correctly might be very simple: cars sold. From the member's point of view, however, how many cars get sold is a means to an end. What does the car salesperson want? Maybe it is simple and extrinsic: commissions. Maybe it is complex and intrinsic: I love being around cars, feeling good about feeding my family, and having first dibs on the new models, *and selling them makes it possible.*

As a member, you must determine what outcomes you want from the high-quality LMX relationship with your leader. These outcomes are your motivation. You might desire concrete things like money or time off, or you may want other things, such as new skills. Whatever it is, it's important to be clear in your mind what you are working toward.

CHAPTER 8

Understanding What Your Leader Needs

The trouble with the world is not that people know too little, but that they know so many things that ain't so.

—MARK TWAIN

The leader's job is to get others to do what the leader needs doing. If you as a member don't know what your team leader needs to get done, then you won't be able to help achieve those goals. A good leader is a good manager and explains what the job is and the expectations around the goal. A SMART goal is a great start on this. However, for this Member Theme, the central question a member must ask is "Why?" rather than "What?" Why is this request important to the leader? Understand the motivation behind the task.

If Morgan requires Alex to make fifteen calls a day, Alex should ask, "Why fifteen?" The answer may be quite clear: fifteen is what has worked in the past and until goals are achieved, that is the standard. Understanding this can help Alex feel better about the fifteen calls and help with the ongoing negotiations about the task at hand.

However, if the reason for that number is unclear, Alex should ask for more information. Successfully asking relies heavily on the current LMX quality. So if Alex doesn't understand why fifteen is magic and asks Morgan, perhaps the answer becomes clearer. "The team isn't meeting its goals, and my boss said to up the call volume. I negotiated to fifteen because I believe that (a) you can do it and (b) it should be enough, in my experience." And maybe even, "My job is on the line here, Alex, and I think fifteen will work. What do you think?" It is beneficial for members to have clarity on what the goal is and why. It's much easier to make each of those calls if you know why you're making them.

SITUATIONS

Here are some examples of how members benefit from knowing what their leader needs from them and knowing the "why."

SITUATION 1: CALL QUOTAS

Morgan as team leader: "Alex, I need you to see more prospects."

Alex thinks, "Why is Morgan asking for this? It's really production that matters. Therefore, I shouldn't just focus on seeing more prospects; I need to see the right prospects. How can Morgan help me see more of the right prospects?" This would be a very healthy out-loud discussion to have.

Members who have a low-quality relationship with their team leader may obediently see more people, because they value being employed. But you look for a better approach, a better way to reach your leader's goal. In a high-quality LMX relationship, you can discuss the situation with your leader and confirm that the "why" is indeed more production. You can suggest to your leader that seeing the right people is more beneficial than focusing on seeing more people. You understand the goal, and you strike a deal to achieve a better outcome.

SITUATION 2: EXPENSE DEADLINES

Morgan: "Each expense must be in within ninety days. If you put any in on day ninety-one or later, you won't get paid for them."

Alex asks, "Why is this deadline important? I'm using my personal credit cards, so why do you care?"

Morgan explains, "The company reports to the shareholders. For that reason, we need to resolve expenses to reflect actual spending in the company. It may just be you on your team with maybe $1,000 of expenses, but there are 5,000 employees in the company. If everybody waited to put everything into accounting, a major shift could occur in our books. This sudden influx of expenses could change our quarterly bottom line, which could affect the stock price. We need to do this to show the reality of our business. My boss educated the managers on that this week."

Alex hadn't ever considered that it's not a personal issue, that there are other factors at play. Alex sees why this is the reason, understands that it is important to Morgan, and is more likely to comply, which is the desired organizational outcome. Alex could also bargain for some clerical help with expenses, explaining that "This would really help the company out!"

SITUATION 3: PUBLIC EVENTS

In this situation, Morgan tells Alex, "We've got a fleet-buyer convention in Orlando coming up. A lot of our customers will be there. I want you to operate our product booth at the event."

Alex is concerned about taking time out of territory. Will sales decline? If their LMX relationship is low quality, Alex might say, "That is not going to increase my production whatsoever. I'd rather not operate the booth." Alternatively, Alex might acquiesce and might even consider that many of the other exhibitors are potential employers, thus exhibiting voluntary termination intention, which is associated with low-quality LMX. (Just a reminder of how important LMX quality is in many subtle ways.)

With a high-quality LMX relationship, Alex might instead say, "Thank you for this opportunity to help the team out. Why is it important that it's me who staffs the booth?" Alex is thinking, "Maybe I can still get out of it."

Morgan clarifies. "We have to have somebody do it, and I thought you would do an excellent job. Frankly, I considered you and four other people for this event. You five are the best on our team of ten. I put the five names in a hat and drew your name. I wish I could tell you it was more scientific than that, but I need you to do this because my boss says we have to have someone represent our product line, and this was the way I thought would be fair and still effective."

This explanation clarifies what is motivating Morgan as the leader and explains why Alex was chosen to help. That doesn't stop Alex from thinking, "I wonder whether I can get a couple days after the convention for some vacation time—hmmm."

SITUATION 4: PRODUCTION GOALS

Morgan tells Alex, "You have $200 in production for Monday. You have $200 carry over from last week. I need another $1,000 by the end of the week." Stunned, Alex asks, "Why?"

"My boss needs $30,000 in total production by that time and will chew me out if that doesn't happen," Morgan explains. "I need to get $4,000 out of my team, so I need you to do this." Alex responds in a high LMX quality way, "Okay, I get it now. Sorry you have that pressure. I know what needs to be done, so I guess I better get on it. I hope we make it."

THE RESULT OF KNOWING WHY

It's important for members to know why they are being asked to do something, but it's also important to solicit that information the right way. You don't want to come across as challenging. Someone could write an entire book on how to pose questions like this, but the central goal is to uncover the "why" without sounding like you disagree.

Managing your leader requires the emotional intelligence

to figure it out on a case-by-case basis. You might say, "Of course I'm going to do as you ask. But it would help me if I understood better why you are asking me to do this. Can you explain your motivation for asking me to accomplish this task?" Knowing the real reason behind something improves your chances of completing the task successfully. When you understand why, you are more likely to take the right action and have better outcomes.

Sometimes you don't want to be the person who's always questioning. With higher-quality LMX relationships, you may trust your leader enough that you don't need to know the whole reason. If your leader is asking you to do something, you trust that it must be important, and that's motivation enough for you. Fulfilling the leader's needs without questioning those requests strengthens the trust and improves the LMX relationship. You should always have the option to ask why. If you don't, that's a sign that you do not have a high-quality LMX relationship.

PERSONAL BENEFITS

When you understand what a leader needs and why, you are in a better position to get what you want. If the leader says, "I need you to do a million dollars in production," you can plan how to negotiate what you want, such as attending that seminar on public speaking. Your desires become part of the negotiation. But remember, you must know what you want and need as well as what your team leader wants and needs and why they need those results.

For example, say you're a jewelry salesperson who is required to work during the end-of-year holidays. Just once you'd like to get two weeks off then, but the rule is clear: no one gets time off between Thanksgiving and New Year's because that is the highest-volume time of the year and the whole team is needed to meet the sales goal. So in January you ask, "If I have met my annual sales goal by November 1 this year, can I have two weeks off around Christmas?"

The leader frowns. This idea isn't flying. "I plan to solve your production issue by meeting my goals early," you point out patiently. "If I meet my goal by November, everything after that is gravy." Now the leader is listening. Leaders enjoy meeting goals early. They savor gravy. Still, the negotiation goes back and forth, and you may not get the two weeks you want. However, you have established some terms to be able to pivot to something else you want, like a summer vacation.

Your ability to reach these personal goals is directly related to the quality of your relationship with your leader. If you get what you want, that's a win, most likely for both of you. Being able to discuss the "why" is a sign you communicate well with your leader. There is mutual trust.

However, you must think about what you want to know and understand what your leader, not your organization, can provide for you. When the leader asks you to staff the booth at the event in Florida, you might negotiate additional time off so you can take your family to Disney World. You each learn what the other finds valuable and confer to make that happen. You both win.

CHAPTER 9

Organizational Citizenship Behavior

Heaven goes by favor; if it went by merit, you would stay out and your dog would go in.

—MARK TWAIN

Organizational citizenship behavior (OCB) is a long name for "helping out." When I first studied this concept, my first thought was "teacher's pet," and to some extent that's correct. OCB is acting in ways not necessarily in your job description to help your leader achieve goals. Understanding your leader's expectations is extremely beneficial, and as a member, you can do even more to achieve a high-quality LMX relationship by exceeding those expectations through a type of volunteerism at work.

All employees have what are known as "in-role" activities—things they must do to accomplish their jobs. But the most successful team members volunteer for "extra-role" activities—work that isn't in their formal job description but helps the team and the leader achieve goals. Sometimes these extra-role behaviors get rolled into a person's job description, but most members who take on extra work are practicing organizational citizenship that pays off with improved relations with their leader.

Organizational citizenship is often misinterpreted. Coworkers might see this behavior of asking to do more of what the leader needs doing as false, self-serving, or calculating. However, if your intent is authentic and genuine, it will improve the LMX relationship with your leader, which is a win. Sometimes you must be intuitive and guess what your leader might like you to do. In a high-quality LMX relationship with reliable communication, the best approach is to ask your leader how you can provide additional help. You may be acting like a teacher's pet, but that is a positive connotation. Your team leader likely will appreciate your offer. Your leader's perception is what matters most because this is about LMX relationship quality.

It's not enough to offer to volunteer, however. You need to do what you say you're going to do. When your leader has accepted your help, you are now in a new task. Make sure you understand what's required, why it is needed, and how you are going to do it. Don't volunteer to do something you don't know how to do. If your leader needs to analyze three new software programs and recommend one, don't raise your hand to help if you understand little about software. Also, make sure you have the time; organizational citizenship can put a strain on your time, finances, and homelife, so carefully weigh the benefits before offering to go above and beyond.

The extra work can be carried out in the same way as in-role tasks are completed. Treat it as part of your regular workload, but make sure that the quality of your extra-role work is as high as your in-role work and that in-role productivity doesn't suffer. Your leader won't appreciate your effort if it's substandard or if it causes you to become unproductive in your regular duties.

As I have already mentioned, be authentic and not manipulative when carrying out extra-role activities. You can't do extra-role work and then immediately turn around and ask for paid vacation days in return. That kind of quid pro quo approach won't enhance your relationship. Your reason for volunteering for extra-role activities is to improve your LMX relationship quality with your leader and foster your leader's trust. Use that trust and bond, not the actual extra-role duties you volunteered for, as leverage for future negotiations.

Here's a personal observation. I am a member of the Harvard Club, a social organization made up of students, graduates, faculty, and parents of students. I volunteer to interview applicants, and when I ask applicants about their volunteer experience, I can tell who is not being sincere and is just padding their resume with volunteer work. I can also perceive when applicants love the volunteer work they do; they display passion and enthusiasm for the work the pretenders simply can't muster. Approach organizational citizenship with the same passion I detect in the successful Harvard College applicants. It's okay to want attention from your leader, but approach extra-role work from a place of wanting to help your leader meet their goals.

For example, I was working for a company that was about to go public, and our accounting division had a lot of work to do. One of the CPAs in my workgroup said, "David, I'd like to help over in the accounting department during this public phase. The work looks interesting, and I'll do it on my own time." Because one of my goals was helping team members improve not only in skills but also in their careers, I said, "If you're getting your work done, I don't have a problem with you doing it. You do great work, and I imagine you can find the time for this."

The head of accounting told me they would need to shift the budget around for this CPA to work extra hours and they didn't have the money, but I offered to pay for it out of my company budget by reducing hours spent in my group. It was unusual to manage this way at the company, but I had what I considered to be a high-quality LMX relationship with this sharp young team member and wanted to help.

After we went public, the CPA transferred departments to become head of corporate relations. All these positive outcomes came out of our one-on-one relationship. Everyone came away happy. Goals, both short and long term, were met.

SITUATIONS

SITUATION 1: UNDESIRABLE TASKS

Salespeople are often asked to evaluate competitors' products and services. This can be time consuming and not particularly enjoyable. As a team member, you can step up and say, "How can I help with this?" A leader can choose to have you help or pass, but in most cases the asking is what counts for improved LMX relationships. The leader can also ask you to do the extra-role task because you are well suited for it. Not all OCB activities are wholly voluntary. Another big subject, *emotional intelligence*, comes into play here in how you react to the request, but that's in other books, such as Daniel Goleman's *Emotional Intelligence*.

Note to team members: keep in mind there needs to be mutual respect regarding organizational citizenship behavior (OCB) in the business world. The leader can ask you to do volunteer work because it will develop you and give you potentially interesting things to do, but if you express your goal of going home at 5 p.m., the leader shouldn't expect more than the negotiated in-role responsibility. Note to leaders: you as the leader can request your team member work on the task during any spare work time they have, but there should not be any punishment because they declined to work beyond what they were supposed to do. Expecting otherwise creates role ambiguity, which is dysfunctional and avoidable.

Role clarity is crucial in this area. If you're looking at this extra task as volunteering, but the leader sees it as part of your job, your role has become ambiguous. This murkiness connects back to the first theme of clarity and understanding what needs to be done and why. This can get confusing, which is why a high-quality LMX relationship is important for you as a team member. It is a good defense.

SITUATION 2: MEANINGFUL VOLUNTEERING

It's tempting to eagerly offer your services whenever a need arises. There are some personality types that consistently exhibit this volunteerism. Leaders are generally aware of what best fits their needs, so a caution is in order if you are a volunteering type. Here's an example: your leader tells the team that they are hiring new people, and a team member immediately says, "I could host a conference call with the new people to help them onboard and answer any questions they may have." A leader might respond in any of the following ways:

- "That would be great. I know they'll need the guidance. It would help me a lot, and I know you would do a good job."
- "I need you to focus on your job. Stay out there and keep hustling. It is my responsibility to guide the new hires."
- "Great idea, but I'm not sure you're the right person for this. Give me some time to think about who is best for this."
- "I already asked our best team member to do it."
- If you're the team member who offered to help, you could feel a little deflated if the response isn't the "yes" you were expecting. It's okay. It is your leader's job to also manage to best results. Volunteering by itself is good, and even a "Thanks, but no thanks" from the leader is positive unless you do it so much and are turned down a lot. Being turned down a lot and not knowing why is indicative of a low-quality LMX relationship, so check yourself on this if needed.

SUMMARY

Social scientists have found a strong positive correlation between LMX quality and organizational citizenship behavior. Although they haven't determined at this time a causal relationship (does one cause the other), that isn't the point. The point is that a fisherman who catches a lot of fish is either a good fisherman or has lots of fish available to catch. Understand that OCB is important, be aware of opportunities, and don't resent being asked to help. That goes a long way in improving LMX relationship quality.

CHAPTER 10

Avoiding Negative Behaviors

A habit cannot be tossed out the window; it must be coaxed down the stairs a step at a time.

—MARK TWAIN

Going above and beyond your regular duties pays dividends in terms of improved LMX relationship quality. It is easy to erode that positive effect through negative behaviors. The negative behaviors in your control appear on the surface to be relatively mild, but in LMX relationship quality terms, these negative behaviors are powerfully caustic. It sounds simple, but it's worth emphasizing: avoid behaviors that annoy your leader. Know what those behaviors are and control how you get into those situations. You need to adopt an attitude to continuously act in ways that never undermine the LMX quality, only improve it.

Be sensitive to what your leader likes and what your leader dislikes. For example, if your leader insists that your "out of office" message on your voicemail and email be, in your opinion, overly detailed, then work together to write one that satisfies this itch. Most leaders make their feelings apparent, so the items on the dislike list should be obvious. Of course, no one wants to anger their leader, but it's also important to avoid even smaller irritations. Mild irritation degrades an LMX relationship the way a fleck of dust makes your eye water.

There are consequences that aren't necessarily related to LMX quality such as the time you were late entering activity, asked for a day off, and were told no. Don't expect to get the day off if your paperwork isn't in—even if your overall relationship with the leader is fantastic. In such cases, you will get a reaction from the leader, hopefully soft, such as the leader saying, "Maybe I didn't express just how important this is." But it may come back to you a little harsher. Avoidance is the best prevention.

If you're getting the idea that nurturing a high-quality leader-member exchange relationship takes work on both sides, congratulations—you are on the right track. Most management books focus on what leaders must do to develop working relationships, but the onus is also on the team member. Going back to the academics, this is a dyad, a pair of people, and because they are people they have personalities. Be aware of your leader's personal likes and dislikes regarding you and your job and you can avoid problems others may have.

TIPS ON NEGATIVE BEHAVIOR AVOIDANCE

1. Find ways to consistently do what your leader wants done in the areas you have identified. Make it as easy on yourself as you can because then you might just do it. For example, you may have come from a company where submitting your expense reports meant sticking your receipts in an envelope and giving them to the accounting department. Now you're at a company where you are required to upload via a smartphone app every receipt contemporaneously with time and date stamps for proof. This system is unfamiliar, but you must change your behavior if your leader makes it clear that it's vital that you do. If altering such behaviors is hard for you, make little reminders for yourself. Put a sticky note on your credit card that you need to take off every time you use it. The message reminds you to take a picture of the receipt as soon as you get it. Make this a good habit.

2. There are explicit and implicit reasons your leader could get upset, and you need to be mindful of both.

Explicit reasons are obvious—the leader voices frustration over someone not turning in activity reports or arriving late to meetings. You see what makes them angry and you understand why. Track what you do regarding those issues. Implicit reasons are harder to ferret out. It just might be a "personal problem" of your leader, but it's still your problem, too.

3. There is the opposite of the halo effect in LMX relationships. Your leader values your association, but if you prove untrustworthy in one area, they may start to question your total reliability. That means lower LMX relationship quality. You can erode the trust within an LMX relationship very quickly.

4. You won't naturally love everything you have to do on the job, but you still should do it. For instance, you might be in a sales job, which offers a base salary plus commission. The commission is easy to get excited about. The base pay is what you get for doing the things you are told to do, such as going to out-of-territory events. Be supportive and do those things. Even if you have no base pay, there is an implicit built-in reward of being employed that is for "just doing your job."

5. You might feel frustrated when you see your leader's boss getting an administrative assistant to do their clerical work. You know their time is valuable, but why doesn't anyone value your time as much? Why is the president of the company flying in a private jet

while you are crammed into economy-minus class? These feelings stem from something called "organizational disconnect." Avoid this trap by letting those feelings go because you can't do anything about the situation. It's okay to talk to your leader about this, of course, but don't make it a big deal if it really doesn't have to be.

If your leader is doing the five behaviors we have talked about, you will have an opportunity to discuss these situations, whether in a formal setting or just over a cup of coffee. With a high-quality LMX relationship, you can talk about these things.

But I do say if the issue is a big deal to you, take it on! Or change jobs, of course, which is high voluntary termination intention, which is associated with low LMX relationship quality. And probably your leader isn't behaving as the chapters earlier suggested. Hey, that would be a good dissertation topic.

SUMMARY

Avoiding negative behaviors ensures that you don't strain the high-quality LMX relationship you have built. This theme isn't as much about constructing that relationship as it is about protecting it. Do the positive things expected of you. Others will regard you as someone who makes your leader look good by doing the things professionally. This positive differentiation from the way others act improves your LMX relationship with your leader and looks good on performance reviews. These actions may not be outstanding behavior on your part; you are just doing your job. However, your leader views your behavior as hugely beneficial. Again, both sides win.

CHAPTER 11

The Journey You've Taken as Leaders and Members

Always do right. This will surprise some people and astonish the rest.

—MARK TWAIN

FOR MEMBERS

For members, I'm not trying to help you get a raise. I'm not trying to get you time off. However, when you have a high-quality LMX relationship, good things will happen. You might get a raise. You might get some extra time off. Social scientists have proven all of this. High-quality LMX relationships reward leaders and members alike. However, you need to constantly improve the LMX relationship quality. You want your leader to count on you and know that you make their life easier.

When you have a high-quality LMX relationship, it becomes much easier to negotiate in the future. You are clearing a path. You may not get anything right away, but when the leader tells you "I owe you one," that's money in the bank. This social exchange seals the trust between you and your team leader, and you'll both continue to be rewarded. It's not a guarantee that nothing will go wrong; plenty of things could happen to throw this off, such as a change in management or resources, so be aware that commitments can change. Nevertheless, improving LMX quality is a worthwhile investment.

You should now have learned that you can create a higher-quality LMX relationship with your leader. It may not be possible in all situations, but I hope you feel more confident about the possibilities. Having a high-quality LMX relationship with your team leader will improve your chances of getting more of what you want out of your employment. Sometimes you don't have a single direct team leader, such as in matrix management. My friend David is a flight attendant and is in this situation. My advice is to still be the best team member possible because you know someone is watching!

The benefits extend beyond the workplace. A rewarding

work life leads to other positive things, such as improved homelife and more satisfying overall experiences.

The central question is this: do you as a member want to enjoy your job more? Here's another crucial question: what outcomes do you want from your work? Decide what those are for you. If you want things to be better, faster, and more efficient, then you now know how to improve your chances of success by working with your leader.

FOR LEADERS

This book isn't a management tome and is not meant to be an academic reference by any means, but it is an exploration of how to achieve goals through higher-quality LMX relationships. For leaders, this process of relationship building is a one-on-one endeavor. You establish the relationships with members one at a time because you want to get outcomes from those members one at a time. It may take a group to accomplish a goal, but that group is made up of individual members, so you need to get these outcomes one member at a time. You must be aware of how you are implementing the five behaviors, checking to see that you are indeed using them and how you use them. Make them habits.

You know how important your work is. You know how much is riding on your success. If you're a leader, your success depends on your team members. Do you think after reading this book that you now have a higher probability of getting done what you need to get done? You should. You only need to implement the behaviors we have discussed. My approach to leadership as a one-on-one sport is proven to be different in outcomes than other leadership styles. Probably the other leadership styles include some of what you have read here, but this book is an explicit description of what you can do that is in your control to make a difference in achieving your goals. You now have a tactical plan to integrate into your career.

A SIMPLE PROCESS

In all five leadership behaviors and all three of the member themes, I have emphasized that you need to identify how to implement them in your own work life. As a leader, how can you integrate Inclusion, Respecting, Rewarding, Improvement, and Modeling? As a member, how do you understand the leader's needs, develop organizational citizenship skills, and avoid negative behaviors and attitudes?

To start, you need to write out SMART goals, something specific, measurable, attainable, relevant, and time bound. Where can you manage yourself strategically and tactically to implement this? Remember to be authentic about your goals, and don't try to force anything.

Then you need to evaluate how you're using the behavior or theme. Decide whether you want to change how you are doing things. Do you feel the need to change? Do you want to get done what you need to get done? Is the situation bad enough that you want to change it?

This change is just implementing actions. It's not about changing who you are. You aren't changing your personality, although that could be an outcome. You might need to change your attitude to become more empathetic, for example, but you must be the one to decide to make that change.

Decide what you want to do, how you are going to do it, and how you're going to measure and evaluate it. Then make the change, measure, and evaluate.

CALL TO ACTION

If this summary makes sense to you, then go out there and do it. If you can implement right away, that's great. If you are hesitant and need to learn more, there are many more resources you can use including Part Four, the toolkit, to follow. Also check in at LMXPro.com, the website for Five Star Leadership®, for current resources to help in understanding the concepts discussed and implementation ideas.

PART FOUR

Toolkit Articles

I've included more material to support what you have already learned. This information is pertinent and useful, but I didn't want to bog you down and have you miss the main points. There will be some repetition to cement these ideas. Please continue to read and learn.

CHAPTER 12

High-Quality LMX Relationships

As a leader with a new team, Morgan is unsure of just how to motivate each member to achieve high individual goals. Alex is of specific concern because although Alex has produced steadily, there hasn't been much growth in production. This year will be a stretch goal for Alex, a situation that can produce dysfunctional anxiety; Morgan will have to manage to that potential problem. Building a high-quality LMX relationship between the two of them is necessary, and fortunately there are proven ways to achieve this, provided they both want it and behave in ways that accomplish higher-quality LMX relationships.

LEADER-MEMBER EXCHANGE: DEEPER BACKGROUND

As noted earlier, the leader-member exchange relationship, or LMX, is a social science construct. A construct is a defined, measurable variable, and LMX is an indicator scored low to high of how well the two parties, the leader and the member, have negotiated a working relationship. It is an exchange relationship, meaning they agree on who gets what and for doing what. The team leader motivates their team member to work; the member gets rewards for doing the work. The rewards can be extrinsic (money) or intrinsic (a job well done, by gosh!) or a combination of extrinsic and intrinsic. Morgan, for example, makes sure the pay scale satisfies team members but also includes job design elements to make the work satisfying itself. Job content is a large subject on its own and deserves attention, especially with today's workers more motivated by intrinsic rewards while still expecting the extrinsic compensation.

MEASUREMENT

The exchange relationship exists; the question social scientists asked was how to measure LMX, because it has at its core complex emotional elements such as trust and respect. Researchers developed ways to measure LMX quality, and there are ongoing new developments, criticism, and theorizing. The challenge is that the process of developing a test requires first deciding what it is to measure; thus, even at the start of the development process, there is disagreement on what the starting point is. An early survey instrument (that's what social scientists call a questionnaire, for example) had just seven questions. The developers called it LMX-7. There was criticism that LMX-7 provided a single answer and did not describe the possible multidimensionality of the LMX relationship. A new survey was designed called LMX-MDM, for multi-dimensionality. It has twelve questions, three for each of four dimensions. To make a long story short, multiple studies have shown that if you want a single answer to the quality question, then either works fine. If you do want to understand subparts of the LMX relationship, then the LMX-MDM, as well as others developed, provides more information. Five Star Leadership® researchers are more interested in the overall quality and use both. Also used are other instruments such as the Empowering Leadership Questionnaire (ELQ) focusing on the single resulting score. We want to see if you are a Five out of Five leader. Do you rate Five Stars?

The questions asked in these instruments include questions something like these:

- Do you know where you stand with your leader or follower?
- Do you usually know how satisfied your leader or follower is with what you do?

- How well does your leader or follower understand your job problems and needs?

These questions may not ask about trust or respect specifically, but they solicit information about the building blocks of the LMX relationship. The answers to these questions fall on a scale, one to five, from "I rarely know how satisfied my leader or follower is with my work" to "Very often I know how satisfied they are" and help determine where a leader and a member stand with one another.

USEFULNESS

The technical definition of an LMX score is the measure of the quality of the working relationship between a supervisor and supervisee (a leader and a follower, a boss and a worker, a team leader and a team member). Most times, LMX scoring is generalized so that it is an overall perception from the viewpoint of the survey taker, which can be the leader or member. Comparing the scores of dyads (the leader vs. the member) can provide good actionable information. A 360-degree development program throws in your peers as well.

It is important to note that although LMX is considered from an overall relationship perspective, the overall perspective consists of many subparts, and these subparts will differ. They differ by the task that the leader and member negotiate. What this means is that the LMX quality can be very high for a negotiated task that is long-standing but very low for a new one. Morgan, for example, may have a high-quality relationship with Alex regarding the sales in Market Niche A (small companies) but a low-quality one for Alex's work in Market Niche B (mid-size companies). This does not mean Morgan distrusts Alex in general or that Alex has no respect for Morgan; it simply means that Morgan doesn't trust Alex to do the work right yet and will have to manage to that. Perhaps from a member point of view, Alex doesn't think Morgan knows much about working mid-size companies but may come to think differently given time and working together in this new market niche.

Trust building can happen slowly or quickly, and the relationship is dynamic. The relationship is created as mental contracts are exchanged between the parties, stating what goals the leader expects the member to accomplish and what will be provided for the worker in terms of resources and compensation. If the member proves the leader wrong by failing to achieve the goals, the LMX quality will likely degrade. That's why some social scientists don't like the scoring methodology at all and would rather use qualitative tools such as diaries and focus interviews to capture the dynamic nature of the LMX relationship. But survey instruments are more prevalent and much easier to administer, especially in the age of SurveyMonkey®.

Working relationships develop over time. Brand-new bosses don't yet have a working relationship with their employees. However, if the boss sits down and says, "How's it going? Tell me about your work," they're already building a relationship that is leader and member based. Getting to know each other is trust building. The member may respond with information about their track record, their recommendations, and their fitness profile, getting the relationship off to a great start. Alternatively, it can be slow going to build the relationship because situations and personalities vary so widely.

As a leader, you seek a greater probability of success; you need to know your team member will accomplish what you've assigned to them and they have agreed to do. LMX quality measurement provides this assurance. Establishing this relationship saves time, effort, worry, and resources. If you know your team member is efficient with their work because you have worked together and have a high-quality relationship, you don't have to be so concerned with managing this person, and you can focus on other things, such as another team member whom you may have a low-quality relationship with. Because you don't have to worry about the first team member, you can afford to spend more time with the second team member making sure they stay focused on the goal. Thus, you spend less time managing while ensuring a higher probability of accomplishing your goals.

CHAPTER 13

Outcomes of
LMX Quality

There are many inputs into creating a high-quality LMX relationship with a team member. The desired main outcome usually is some sort of production goal achievement. It turns out that along the way to goal achievement, LMX relationship quality is associated with other outcomes—high quality with more positive outcomes and fewer negative outcomes and the inverse. These other outcomes are very important to total organizational behavior, sometimes more important than goal achievement. See what you think.

LMX QUALITY AND SYNERGY

High-quality LMX relationships create synergy. A leader

can create team synergy through building high-quality LMX relationships one team member at a time. The outcome is more than the ability to work together; there will be much shared in terms of commitment, talent, and interests. With synergy, the team gets more done with fewer resources, which should lead to greater reward. Maybe the leader helps team members finish a job, get paid, and go home earlier. Maybe they get more money, extra time off, better training, or more frequent work parties. If the member gets what they want, they're going to be more satisfied with the working relationship. A high-quality LMX relationship creates more for both parties: the member gets more of what they want out of the job, and the leader knows they have a higher probability of getting the job done right with less work.

Let's make Morgan a Pit Crew Chief in a car racing company. Consider how Morgan manages the Pit Crew including the Tire Passer, Inside Front Tire Changer, "Dead Man," Fueler, Starter/Tire Passer, Inside Rear Tire Changer, Fire Extinguisher, and the Jack Man. When the race is on the line and fractions of a second matter, the Pit Crew members do their magic, and Morgan as Chief observes the well-trained Crew. Morgan's team has trained so well that Morgan trusts each member to do what's needed to achieve the goal, which is to get their car back out on the track in ten seconds or less. That accomplishment is through synergy. It is highly likely

Morgan has a high-quality LMX relationship with each team member.

The goal is measurable—the team has ten seconds to get the car on the track. The Crew Chief and each Pit Crew member understands the importance of this goal because they know races are won by fractions of a second. How does each team member know what to do? It's not because Pit Crew Chief Morgan has announced it at a team meeting. It's because Morgan has worked with each team member individually to make sure that the people changing the tires, the person adding the fuel, and everyone else accomplishes their assigned tasks so that they add up to the overall goal.

From the team member's point of view, they get what they desire from accomplishing the goal. Perhaps they want to be appreciated and recognized, and after a job well done, Morgan tells them, "Good job. You changed the tires faster than ever before." Maybe each member gets a $5,000 bonus as part of the racer's winnings, which gives them the incentive to be the fastest pit crew. Or it could be as simple as completing their first race without any mechanical issues. Whatever each member wants out of their job, they have a greater chance of receiving those rewards if they have figured out one-on-one with their leader what exactly is expected in their part of the job.

The leader then makes sure every other member is on the

same page, and members can have input in this area to help the team. Max, the expert tire changer, might realize that Harper on the front driver's side is the slowest at changing a tire. Max could say to Morgan, "Should I show Harper how to get this done faster?" In this case, Max voluntarily exhibits what is called organizational citizenship to help the leader get the job done, a good outcome of high-quality LMX relationships.

LOWER VOLUNTARY TURNOVER AND LMX

Another positive outcome of having high-quality LMX relationships is lower voluntary turnover. Not only will fewer people quit, but there will also be fewer negative behaviors that are proven to be associated with people thinking about quitting. When someone considers quitting, they start exhibiting voluntary termination intention, or VTI. The more they think about leaving, the more they do the things that aren't necessarily what the leader wants. VTI might show up as heavier drinking, drug abuse, tardiness, absenteeism, being a pain in the butt at work, and, of course, lower job performance.

In the social sciences, we describe intentions as planned behaviors, to which we can give a grade. Low intention means the outcome is unlikely to happen. People with low VTI are very satisfied. They aren't thinking, "I hate my boss," "Man, I don't want to do that extra assignment," or "God, I wish I had a drink." With low VTI, you avoid those negative thoughts and actions.

High VTI means these negative thoughts take over and spur the ultimate action—the employee quits. This may seem like the worst-case scenario, but it's not. You may have an even bigger problem on your hands if someone who hates the job stays in it because they need the money or medical insurance, or whatever their reason. A high need to stay combined with a high desire to leave leads to nothing but trouble. High VTI can also be prevented with high-quality LMX relationships that, through appropriately applied leader behaviors, resolve this challenge one way or another. To really cement this idea that this can be a problem, "going postal" can be a signal of very high VTI in the shooter.

ROLE CONFLICT AND AMBIGUITY

Team members can develop bad attitudes resulting in low productivity and other negative outcomes due to *role conflict* and *role ambiguity*. Role conflict is when a worker has two things to do, but they conflict with each other, and the worker is not able to do both successfully. Role ambiguity means that the worker does not know what they are supposed to be doing; the opposite is *role clarity*. How does LMX relationship quality apply, and how can high-quality relationships overcome these problems?

In role conflict, people know what their job is but can't accomplish one goal without sacrificing another. For example, Alex's task for the day is to make forty house calls, but there is a committee meeting about the dress code on the schedule that is important to Morgan, Alex's team leader. Alex is faced with a decision with no clear winner—miss some appointments, miss the committee meeting, or be resigned to working longer hours. That creates a conflict between Alex's two tasks, and this also conflicts with what Alex wants out of work. If the situation remains unresolved, nobody, including Morgan, will be satisfied. Resolving the problem requires a high-quality LMX relationship between Alex and Morgan with the use of relations-oriented leader behaviors such as Inclusion. The trust and respect will find a win-win solution.

The same applies to role ambiguity. High-quality LMX relationships are built on the premise of shared agreement of what needs to be done and how to do it. Ambiguity creates tension in the team member and makes good outcomes from the task less likely. If there is ambiguity, a shared understanding of the task hasn't been negotiated. For example, Alex is tasked with preparing a market survey, a new experience. Morgan needs to check with Alex on whether there is an understanding of the work and whether they find there is role clarity. They can come to an agreement to avoid potential problems. This discussion requires the use of the relations-oriented leader behaviors. Addressing role conflict and role ambiguity using quality-improving behaviors is good leadership.

OUTCOMES FOR LEADERS

Leaders need to accomplish their goals. The functional outcome an organization seeks is to get more at less cost, or, in a word, productivity. With efficient and effective team members who are motivated to play a part in productivity, leaders will achieve their own goals, and this should add up to achieving the organization's goals. The main requirement is that the leader's goals get met.

This book's job is not to figure out what a leader's goals are. You, as a leader and manager, need to be able to set goals, allocate resources, and motivate your team members so they can be efficient and effective to meet your goals. With this sort of team in place, meeting goals will be easier because you will generate more money or more time. With an efficient team, you will be more likely to have more of both money and time. Using knowledge of how to improve LMX quality one-on-one with each team member leads to a better leader experience.

OUTCOMES FOR MEMBERS

To nurture high-performing team members, leaders need to know what members want out of their jobs and what is in their leader's power to provide. Team member desires fall into three categories: more money, more time, and more development.

- More money: If a member has a great relationship with their leader, the member may get more sales territory, which would result in more money. Maybe the member gets a bonus structure that differs from everyone else's, if HR allows that. Science shows that leaders shift resources to those team members they have higher-quality LMX relationships with, whether consciously or subconsciously.
- More time: If a member has a high-quality LMX relationship with their leader, then the leader and member can negotiate the task environment of the work to free up time for the member. Research suggests that if a member can negotiate openly with their leader, then tasks can be eliminated that do not directly affect productivity. An example would be asking for and getting additional internal sales support for the territory.
- More development: Many members want more and better learning opportunities. If there is a high-quality LMX relationship with the leader, the member is more likely to get those developmental desires fulfilled. The LMX relationship provides openness to discuss what the member would want or need while allowing their leader to temper the discussion with what is possible.

Meeting members' needs is a very individualized process. We know that leaders are more likely to provide the member who has a high-quality LMX relationship something they have the authority to provide.

Creating a higher-quality LMX relationship with your team leader is simple—find out what your team leader needs and then do it. I'm surprised at how many people don't understand that. You won't develop a high-quality LMX relationship with your team leader if you fail to get the required reports in and then you are called out on it in a meeting. You could make your leader's life much easier if you just handed in the reports. I see situations like this, and I wonder, "Why are you arguing about sending in your reports? Just do it." Be proactive in improving the LMX quality.

To understand your leader's needs, it is helpful to ask privately, "Why do you need these reports sent by a certain time?" The response might be, "It's because my boss is on my butt about it, so please do it for me." Conversations like this improve LMX relationship quality.

NEXT CHAPTER

By now, it's becoming clear that the one-on-one relationships make all the difference in meeting business goals. Many management and leadership books focus on the relationship between a leader and a group of followers, which is fine as far as it goes. Leadership, though, is ultimately a one-on-one sport, and I will teach you how to excel in that sport.

CHAPTER 14

The One-on-One Relationship

The one-on-one characteristic of team leadership is central to LMX relationships. That is what is being improved through the leader and member behaviors. How does Morgan handle this?

Morgan's sales team goal has increased 50 percent over last year. Morgan is evaluating the team, thinking, "I have ten team members. Five are pretty good and will do fine with this goal, but the other five are borderline. I need to get the borderline ones up to full speed for us to achieve that new goal."

At this point, Morgan needs a good angel to say, "You know, there's that thing called high-quality LMX relationships you heard about at that seminar. Maybe you should try that."

Being a wise leader, Morgan says, "You know, darn it, that's what I need to do. Yes, I must think about the team, but I also need to develop a one-on-one relationship with each member so each individual succeeds, and that will lead to team success."

GETTING STARTED

Morgan can now start to consider how to develop those relationships. Realizing that each team member is thinking, "I'm not particularly concerned with anyone else. I care about how I can succeed and have the job I want this year," Morgan must shift perspective to focus on what each individual wants to motivate them to achieve the new goal. Up until now, it's highly likely Morgan has been successful but not entirely aware of how it's happening. That's called unconscious competence. Morgan may already be doing some of the things we're about to discuss but being unconsciously competent is not nearly as effective as being consciously competent, because you improve what you measure, and to measure, you must recognize it.

The paradigm Morgan has worked under, which has been reasonably successful, is to manage the team's activity to results. Morgan has read *The Seven Habits of Highly Effective People* by Covey and *The New One Minute Manager* by Blanchard and Johnson but wants more than those books provided. Morgan wants to consciously improve the total results, but though unconscious competence has carried the day in some basic leadership areas, tactically doing those things that bring behaviors to consciousness is the way to success. The situation can't be improved enough by delivering collective pep talks and congratulating the team. Morgan needs to think less in terms of "How do I manage the team to success?" and more in terms of "How do I lead the individual members to success so that it adds up to team success?"

In my career, I have had experiences where a boss managed the team, but nobody on the team had a one-on-one relationship with management. I have also had team leaders who created that one-on-one relationship with each team member. Both approaches achieved success, but I was happier with the latter. You need to buy into the idea that behaving as a leader can be consciously applied to improve outcomes such as sales team goal achievement.

THE ONE-ON-ONE SPORT

LMX, as we are talking about it, is the leader's exchange relationship with each team member. This is a special relationship not necessarily based in being best friends.

Leadership is a one-on-one sport where leaders motivate groups of people by appealing to individuals. They don't attempt to appeal to the group mind in this case but to a team of individuals who happen to start thinking the same way. This then leads to group activity and goal achievement.

It is possible to lead by selecting only some members for improved LMX quality activities, sometimes called the "in-group," but it is true leadership when applied to all members of the team. Morgan can't just say to the team, "We've got to do a million in production. Five of you are on track for your goals, but the other five need to step it up." This isn't leadership. Morgan probably won't change the behaviors of the five underperforming members much with this approach. There are many reasons a team member may be stuck at a certain level, and group exhortation does not remedy these.

Instead, Morgan needs to treat each person as an individual team member and consciously work with them in that way. This outreach must involve more than just words. Morgan can tell every team member that they are valued and cared for, but caring is not a behavior. It is a description of a set of behaviors, and a leader needs to discern the correct behaviors for everyone individually. You care about them, yes, but are you caring for them correctly in terms of improved LMX quality?

COACHING EACH INDIVIDUAL

Each one-on-one relationship will differ to be effective because we're all unique. If you're familiar with tests like the Myers-Briggs Type Indicator, you've gotten a glimpse of the complexity of our makeup. The Myers-Briggs personality test describes four characteristics that combine into sixteen differing personality types—quite complex, and yet those are just general characteristics. You better expect each leader-member relationship to manifest differently. And remember, as a leader, if you relate correctly with individual team members to produce high-quality LMX relationships, you're more likely to get the desirable outcomes. This is worth the effort.

Not only does the leader need to recognize character traits of the members, but members need to recognize characteristics of their leaders as well. If you've changed jobs or there's been a switch in management at your current job, you probably won't be able to interact with your new leader the same way as you did the previous and expect the same results. The new leader isn't necessarily better or worse than the other, but they most definitely will be different.

Maybe it comes as a surprise, but a team is just a group of individuals. For this reason, this one-on-one approach to motivating group behavior is so effective. You can aggregate it into team behavior, but at the microlevel, you need to connect with how an individual is motivated to act so their actions add to team results.

The modern Marine boot camp provides another excellent example. In twelve weeks, the Marine Corps forms a relationship with new members, first with their Drill Instructor, who ensures they will do what the DI as team leader wants them to do, when the leader wants them to do it, and exactly how it should be done. They then create institutional loyalty, a subject of immense value but beyond this book's purpose, by imbuing each recruit with the characteristics to succeed in the field. The best leaders don't beat the individualism out of their recruits; they create in the Marine an individual relationship with the greater organization that the Marine will now follow through intense individual attention during boot camp.

CAREFUL WHAT YOU ASK FOR

If you're going to ask your team to accomplish more, you better make sure you know what you want to accomplish. Therefore, management is still important. If you're a good leader but a bad manager, you will get results, but they will likely be the wrong results. For example, if your sales manager says, "It is important to see as many people a week as you can. If you see forty people a week, you'll be a success," that's probably not enough information. If the manager doesn't inform the team members that the sales goal is $1 million and doesn't check on how they are doing, they might make the forty calls without knowing how much they need to sell.

A great leader can get each member to do forty calls a week as requested; a great leader and manager will get them to do the calls and achieve the sales goal. Make sure you are a great manager first. Then add one-on-one leadership to give yourself a greater chance of achieving the bottom-line goals.

Leadership results in greater management success. Management alone is helpful, but adding leadership allows you to gain better results from the same effort. Leadership makes it easier for management to succeed.

NEXT CHAPTER

So much in your business life is out of your control, but in this book, we talk about the things you can control. If you recognize the difference, you can focus on the behaviors under your control that are most likely to produce results.

In the next chapter, we review the specific behaviors that have been proven to improve the one-on-one LMX relationships. There are many things you can do, but we will be focusing on the five leader behaviors you can control as a leader and three ways you can help improve LMX as a member. You don't even have to let anyone know you're doing them; they'll still work.

Any leader who wants to get better results knows the frustration of knocking down the pins one at a time and always being left with one that just won't fall—something you need to get permission to do. I want to help you get rid of all the noise in your head and focus on the things you don't need permission to do—actionable things that affect what is missing in one-on-one relationships. These strategically implemented behaviors will help you lead your team to success.

CHAPTER 15

What Can Be Controlled

Sometimes you are limited as a leader. You inherited a team, but some members aren't succeeding. You need rewards to motivate them, but you don't have the budget. You need to put those limitations in the closet and move on. As the saying goes, you need to accept the things you cannot change, have courage to change the things you can, and have wisdom to know the difference. Let's talk about what can be controlled.

THE QUEST FOR HIGH-QUALITY RELATIONSHIPS

Morgan now understands the importance of one-on-one relationships. At this point, however, Morgan doesn't recognize what can or can't be controlled. Making that determination isn't always easy. Morgan's boss, for instance, is kind of a jerk who hasn't involved Morgan in any of the decision making. The boss isn't moving an inch on the sales goal, so that is nonnegotiable. The company needs a 50 percent increase this year. Also, there is no telling whether the economy will rise or tank. All these things are out of Morgan's control, so they must be put in the closet.

FIVE LEADERSHIP BEHAVIORS

The goal of Five Star Leadership® is to provide a platform for a leader to implement five specific behaviors. Implementing these behaviors is a tactic to employ to better the chances of achieving goals. As a reminder, these are as follows:

- **Inclusion** means authentically involving a member in decision making regarding aspects of their work.
- **Respecting** is demonstrated when a leader acknowledges that each team member is an individual with feelings, problems, and goals of their own.
- **Rewarding** is acknowledging superior results with something of value (intangible or tangible) to the member.
- **Improvement** means actively helping a team member get better at something, whether job related or not.

- **Modeling** is how strong leaders exhibit the attitudes and behaviors they would like members to exhibit and show them how to succeed in their jobs.

For Morgan to fully utilize these leadership behaviors, there will need to be a strategic and tactical plan to implement them. This requires objective observation of current behavior, and conscious implementation of change, measurement, and analysis. We know where Morgan needs to go in the long run: higher LMX quality scoring with each team member. This scoring can be done with the LMX-7 instrument, for example, as a self-check. Or a more formal program can be put in place. The instrument is copyrighted, so I don't provide it here, but Google "LMX-7 people.Uncw.edu" and you will find it.

LMX QUALITY IS TASK-DEPENDENT

One characteristic of LMX relationships that is often not clear is that you and your team member will have a higher-quality relationship concerning one task than you do another task. For example, Andy, a vehicle sales manager, regards Haley as the best pickup truck seller on the team. Andy trusts Haley to keep it up, and the LMX relationship is probably high quality. However, if Andy transfers Haley to the "male middle-age crisis sports car" sales group, Andy doesn't know exactly how well Haley will do with the different line, so the new task-dependent

LMX relationship starts with lower quality. This isn't bad; it's a fact of how LMX works. Although it isn't a high-quality LMX relationship yet regarding the new position, it has a great foundation for becoming one based on the existing LMX relationship about truck sales. Andy knows Haley can sell trucks well, so the existing trust and respect are a great starting point to transfer this high LMX quality to the new task. There is a halo effect.

One question that comes up often is whether all tasks are considered important for LMX relationship quality. Nope. The difference in importance is based on how structured the task is. A "structured" task is something that is specifically described, as in a manual, so that a person can be managed to do the task as instructed. An "unstructured" task is one where the leader and member must agree upon who is going to do what, how, etc. LMX relationship quality is much more important in unstructured tasks. The leader and member decide what needs to be done, how to do it, who will do what, what resources are required, and what the rewards are. Unstructured tasks may be relatively simple; when done often enough, they appear to be structured tasks, but that is only because the negotiations are done, and the work is going well. Transferring the task to a different team member, though, will likely show that the task is still unstructured as the new member to the task learns the ropes and the LMX quality improves.

Imagine Andy as team leader asking Haley (of vehicle sales fame), "How do you plan on achieving your sales goals this year?" Andy is already establishing an unstructured task by asking, "How are you going to do it?" rather than saying, "Here's the manual, now get to work."

Haley replies, "I'm going to make forty calls a day to previous customers and referrals." Andy disagrees and counsels, "Forty may not be enough. In my experience, you will need to do sixty. You know it takes an average of eight calls just to get the prospect on the phone!" This short dialogue emphasizes the importance of the question "How well do you think your leader understands your job?" to LMX relationship quality. They are negotiating how to get this job done.

There probably are situations where everything is structured and there is little need for a team leader to be concerned with LMX relationship quality. I have not studied these nor been employed in such a job. Even selling newspaper subscriptions door-to-door was unstructured. Repossessing cars was highly unstructured despite the FTC and GMAC rulebooks. The financial services industry with the SEC and FINRA making rules does not create structure at the sales team level. What I am saying is assume LMX relationship quality is important and behave as a leader.

SUMMARY

Leaders need to create a strategic plan to implement each of the five behaviors. As a leader, you need to know what the behaviors are, of course, but you also need to evaluate how you are going to use these behaviors. You need to decide whether you want to implement them or whether you want to modify them to fit a certain environment, relationship, or personal preference. If you do decide to change them, what changes are you going to make, and why do those changes make sense for the relationship you have in mind?

As a leader, you probably recognize this decision-making process. It's the kind of process good managers use when strategizing. Keep that in mind; to become a leader, you must manage yourself from time to time.

CHAPTER 16

Graduation

Thank you for reading about this great subject, leadership. Even anarchists have teams, and they need leadership; the structure just isn't hierarchical. Leadership exists on the playing field where the team "captain" really isn't in charge of anything, and the real leaders may be other players or the coach. Leadership can rotate as it does in Scouts. Leaders are probably members of a team with a leader.

The goal of this book was to connect the dots that science has shown connect. The dots include the team leader, the team member, the tasks, the resources, the compensation, the extra-role activities, the non-role-specific behaviors, and many more. Connecting these dots is the LMX relationship. Other connections exist and coexist with LMX quality. Understanding the significant role LMX relationship quality has in organizational behavior means you understand the following:

1. Keeping LMX quality in the forefront as a key measure for success increases the likelihood of good things happening and bad things not. This is true for both members of the dyad, the team leader and team member.
2. Knowing as a team leader what goals need achieving and being able to describe them to the team members creates an outcome target that can be measured. Use SMART goals.
3. Leaders can change their input to the LMX relationship quality score by behaving in five distinct, learnable, measurable ways: Inclusion, Respecting, Rewarding, Improvement, and Modeling.
4. Members can consciously act to understand a leader's needs, perform extra-role activities, and avoid annoying their leader, which leads to improved LMX relationship quality.
5. Change is actionable: it is identifiable, learnable, and measurable. But just as it takes only one psychologist to change a lightbulb, the lightbulb must want to change.

Good luck on your journey and let me know at david-smith@oafound.org how I can help.

Acknowledgments

After all the writing and editing, what comes to mind is Willie Nelson and Julio Iglesias singing "To All the Girls I've Loved Before." In case you don't know the words, here are the first three lines:

To all the girls I've loved before
Who traveled in and out my door
I'm glad they came along

I acknowledge all the bosses and coconspirators I have known through the years. Most have retired by now, and that is too bad in some cases. Maybe some might buy this book and recognize themselves, if they remember me at all. I remember all of them.

About the Author

In addition to my Doctor of Philosophy degree in organizational leadership, I have forty years of experience on financial services sales teams. I have two master's degrees and four industry designations from that career. I have had a great career with many team leaders and team members in sales of financial services products.

I live in La Costa, California, with my wife, Dr. Anna Smith. She has earned her Doctor of Acupuncture and Chinese Medicine, which she pursed after a career in nursing as a registered nurse, patient education with her master's in public health, and many years as a medical massage specialist. She is on the professorial staff at a graduate school in San Diego.

When we aren't working, we enjoy camping in our So-Cal Teardrop trailer we named Matilda. I once saw a trailer that had a bumper sticker saying, "I go where I'm towed," and that's what Matilda does. We go to comfortable campgrounds where we can stretch out and recharge. Matilda recharges with us, soaking up the sun through her solar charger.

I am a PADI open water scuba instructor, and though I've been diving in northern Massachusetts and here in California, most of my diving is in warm water now. I love Cozumel and Bonaire.